Rooted
in the Earth

Rooted
in the Earth

RECLAIMING
THE AFRICAN AMERICAN
ENVIRONMENTAL
HERITAGE

Dianne D. Glave

Lawrence Hill Books

Library of Congress Cataloging-in-Publication Data

Glave, Dianne D.
Rooted in the earth : reclaiming the African American environmental heritage /
Dianne D. Glave. — 1st ed.
p. cm.
Includes bibliographical references and index.
ISBN 978-1-55652-766-1 (pbk.)
1. African Americans—History.   2. African Americans—Social conditions.
3. Indigenous peoples—Ecology—United States.   4. Human beings—Effect of
environment on—United States.   5. Environmentalism—United States.
6. Environmental justice—United States.   I. Title.
E185.G54 2010
305.896'073—dc22
2010008130

An earlier version of chapter 9, "Women and Gardening: A Patch of Her Own,"
appeared in *Environmental History* in July 2003. An earlier version of chapter
10, "Environmental Justice: Free to Breathe," appeared in *Griot: The Journal of
Black Heritage* in November 2005.

Cover design: Rachel McClain
Cover photo: © UpperCut Images / Getty Images
Interior design: Pamela Juárez

Lawrence Hill Books is an imprint of
Chicago Review Press, Incorporated
814 North Franklin Street
Chicago, Illinois 60610

ISBN 978-1-55652-766-1
Printed in the United States of America

Dedicated to the memory of my grandparents,
Gladys Yates and Cyril and Christine DePass,
and to Basil DePass, Clifford DePass, Clayton DePass,
and Rona Smellie, my uncles and aunt.

Sometimes I think: I am older than this tree, older than this bench, older than the rain. And yet. I'm not older than the rain. It's been falling for years and after I go it will keep on falling.

—NICOLE KRAUSS, *THE HISTORY OF LOVE*

Contents

Preface

Three little birds
Pitch by my doorstep
Singin' sweet songs
Of melodies pure and true

—BOB MARLEY, "THREE LITTLE BIRDS"

My personal journey to environmental awareness began in the borough of Queens and later led to a bend of the Mississippi River in New Orleans and on to metro Atlanta. I grew up near John F. Kennedy Airport in Rosedale, New York, my beloved neighborhood of concrete, asphalt, ranch homes, and rumbling planes, with my immediate family: my parents, Daphne and Percy Glave, and my brother, Richard Glave.

During those early years and continuing into my adulthood, I often sprawled out on my parents' bed or sat at their kitchen table, listening to them reminisce about Jamaica, their first home, their "old country," defined for some by Bob Marley and his music. They spoke of my grandparents, born in the 1890s, who lived indirectly and directly off Jamaica's reddish-brown claylike soil, much like the farmers who cultivated the land in the American South.

Boss Yates, Percy's stepfather, made his living as an agent for a purchasing association, acting as an intermediary between local banana farmers and international buyers. He married Gladys Gibson, my grandmother.

My mother's parents, Cyril and Christine DePass, owned a small farm in Halifax, Manchester, Jamaica, at a distance from their home, where they grew coffee and bananas while fattening pigs, chickens, and cows for slaughter. I traveled to the farm as a child during the 1960s. I remember arriving by plane to visceral smells, vistas, and tastes so different from those of New York. On humid afternoons, perspiration covered my neck as I rode a donkey, witnessed a hog bloodily slain and butchered, and peered at yams, potatoes, bananas, and coffee growing in the yard. Water was piped into the house from a nearby well that was filtered by small golden fish. Delicate green lizards flitted about the yard.

My parents launched my informal nature study during the 1970s when they drove Richard and me to Baker's Camp in upstate New York for our annual weeklong summer vacations. I swam, fished, and rowed on the lake. Early in the day, I would crawl past the slippery lichen-covered walls of Dead Man's Cave and wander below the shadowed understory of the woods. In the afternoons, I chased deer and chipmunks under and over downed trees, and by evening, I would be sitting on the pier by the lake, kicking my feet, baiting my hooks with worms, and catching and tossing back sunnies—small rainbow-colored fish.

I was similarly awed by New Orleans, where I revised parts of this book. This mystifying emerald of a spot on the Mississippi River teemed with snowy egret at the water's edge and with black swallowtail butterflies, lime green lizards, and weighted banana trees in the city. In the French Quarter, palmetto bugs—giant winged roaches—crawled along the damp walls. In New Orleans I lived at the mercy of rain, humidity, and wind. I watched the sky for darkened clouds.

I fled from hurricanes. My memory of my time there is bittersweet since I escaped Hurricane Katrina but left behind a city of people who were very kind to me.

More recently, I have lived and completed this book in three spots in Georgia: Stone Mountain, midtown Atlanta, and East Point. These areas, though parts of a sprawling metropolis with cars and people speeding to and fro, are dotted with tranquil parks and skirted by the wilderness of state parks. New Orleans and Atlanta called to me like old friends, the former with its lingering African influences and the latter with its sizable population of Caribbean immigrants. Even in these primarily urban settings, I have found ways to explore and enjoy the nature around me to feed my soul and my senses. I urge people everywhere, especially African Americans, to do the same.

Rooted in the Earth

Introduction

PEOPLE AND CURRENTS

He inquired if I did not want to take farming. I told him promptly that I had worked enough on a farm and did not care to learn anything more about it. He then asked me if I would like to take agriculture. I said that I thought I would like that very well. So he assigned me to the livestock division. Imagine my surprise when I learned that agriculture was farming.

—THOMAS MONROE CAMPBELL, ON SELECTING
CLASSES AT TUSKEGEE INSTITUTE, *THE MOVABLE SCHOOL
GOES TO THE NEGRO FARMER*, 1936

Stereotypes persist that African Americans are physically and spiritually detached from the environment. This wrongheaded notion is so ingrained in our culture that many of us have begun to believe it ourselves. But nothing could be less true. From ancient Africa to the modern-day United States, people of African descent have continued the legacy of their relationship with the land.

3

This book explores the history of environmental activities and attitudes in the African American community and asks: Did Africans and the enslaved espouse and practice some form of environmentalism, and can some preliminary parallels be drawn between these practices and those of free African Americans? What did nature mean to African Americans? Did religion and spirituality inform their interpretations of nature? How did African Americans practice agricultural methods and soil conservation techniques? How did African American women embrace the aesthetics and conservation of gardening? In what ways did African Americans practice preservation? What were children's experiences in rural environmentalism? What are the contemporary parallels in Africa and the United States?

Many African Americans, including historic figures like Thomas Monroe Campbell, the first black federal agricultural agent, have long expressed their ambivalence about the land. Campbell's feelings about farming, expressed in the epigraph to this chapter, were formed and hardened during his time as a sharecropper and day laborer. Those feelings were negative, and for good reason, since he performed labor that he considered demeaning and that originated in the arduous work of enslaved people in Southern society. At the Tuskegee Institute, Campbell agreed to take an agriculture class, believing that agriculture translated into upward mobility toward middle-class African American ranks. Farming, on the other hand, seemed to him to be a step down into life among the black masses.

Such feelings of distaste are long-standing for African Americans whose forefathers and -mothers experienced nature entwined with fear and violence. Stories of the horrors and hardships of the Middle Passage, passed from generation to generation through oral tradition, created anxiety long after our ancestors had completed their arduous journeys. The sick and infirm were thrown overboard, and seasickness was common in the stifling, unsanitary holds belowdecks. This was true for Olaudah Equiano, an African from Benin who was enslaved and forced to leave Africa for the Americas. For others, like Joseph Cinque, a West African who was transported to the Americas on the slave ship the *Amistad*, the Atlantic Ocean was a stage for violence. Cinque, along with his fellow Africans, revolted against Spanish enslavers on the ship. Runaway slaves experienced dread of being tracked and captured by whites in woods and swamps in the Americas. Perhaps even worse were memories of whites taking land away from free African Americans through taxation and the withholding of government loans.

In the years after enslavement, African Americans began to move to Northern cities in a series of mass migrations that continued into the 1970s. This relocation to the increasingly urbanized North distanced them from the rural experiences of their parents and grandparents, who lived and worked in fields, gardens, and woods. Scorn, distaste, and fear of nature became the emotional legacy of a people who had been kidnapped from their homelands and forced to make the long journey across the Atlantic Ocean to pick cotton and prime tobacco for often violent and abusive masters; they were finally subjected to losing legally owned land to the whites who continued to victimize them long after slavery was banned.

Were these terror-filled experiences passed to future generations, though only the essence of the original stories remained? Did they leave behind a shapeless, lingering fear, manifested today among urban African Americans? The answer to these questions is undoubtedly yes, as the legacy of these historical experiences has hardened into yet another stereotype: the ambivalent or apathetic environmentalist, or even the antienvironmentalist. This stereotype is embraced even by African Americans themselves. So one more image has been added to the sambo, sapphire, coon, and mammy, all originating in enslavement and perpetuated today.

Though there is some truth in the antienvironmentalist stereotype, the reality is more complex. African Americans have long envisioned the environment in luminous and evocative ways, while at the same time remaining pragmatic and realistic about the wilderness. Only recently have African Americans been considered in the study of environmental history—a history traditionally defined as by and for white men. But things are slowly changing, and now we can look to African Americans like Campbell, who yearned for upward mobility and found it in federal government agricultural reform, as a rich and integral part of that history.

Contemporary novelist, poet, essayist, and farmer Wendell Berry broadly defines two strands of environmentalism. The first is preservation in what some would consider wild places, like the ocean, the woods, and swamps. The second is conservation of natural resources, including the land, water, forests, and minerals. Early twentieth-century white environmentalists generally faced off along these distinct lines of preservation versus conservation. Today preservation takes the form of caring for natural areas, such as state parks like Yosemite. An example of conservation is using windmills—rather than dwindling petrofuels—to provide energy.

At the same time and alternately, some rural African Americans and whites who were not formally part of this national environmentalist movement learned and applied both preservationist and conservationist ideologies and practices—a preservation-conservation, for lack of a better term.

For example, a farmer's son could spend his summer at a conference, learning about moths and butterflies—education as a means of connecting to nature through preservation—and then return home to spread fertilizer in a field in preparation for planting, practicing a form of conservation that protected and enhanced the soil.[1]

George Washington Carver, Ned Cobb, and Thomas Monroe Campbell are all distinctive voices in an expansive environmental history, reflections of preservation-conservation defined and practiced by African Americans. Their words embody the rhetoric of early twentieth-century environmentalism. Carver and Cobb drew on preservation-conservation to imbue nature with human characteristics while also exploiting the environment for economic gain.

Carver, a director of the Tuskegee Experiment Station, did not divide preservation and conservation but instead entwined the two. He advocated for protection of, or "justice" for, the soil in nature in the tradition of preservation. He also experimented with crops using the soil. He mused,

> Unkindness to anything means an injustice done to that thing. If I am unkind to you I do you an injustice, or wrong you in some way. On the other hand, if I try to assist you in every way that I can to make a better citizen and in every way to do my very best for you I am kind. The above principles apply with equal force to the soil.

The farmer Ned Cobb, whose oral history *All God's Dangers: The Life of Nate Shaw* describes his life as an Alabama farmer, also gave the land human qualities, using metaphors of preservation and conservation. "It injures your land to plow it wet, it injures your crop," said Cobb. "Pile up wet earth around the stalks, it dries and scalds 'em out."[2] Cobb gave the business of farming some humanity.

Southerners painting a romanticized picture of nature to entice African Americans to remain in the South rather than migrate north were, according to Thomas Monroe Campbell, "wont to picture to [migrants] the beauties of nature, the golden sunset, the babbling brooks, and the singing birds. But all of these have little of beauty and grandeur to the Negro farmer, who is constantly in debt, hungry, sick and cold, and without civil protection."[3] Interestingly, Campbell's own memoir reveals that he valued nature when it served the personal, economic, and political needs of African Americans, like himself, who tilled or taught others to cultivate Southern soil.

What makes the environmental experience of African Americans distinctive? Enslaved people did not stumble upon or discover wilderness. Instead, African Americans actively sought healing, kinship, resources, escape, refuge, and salvation in the land. The environment held social meaning for enslaved people. Contrary to the dominant purist sort of preservation that emphasized places and not people—the practice and ideology of whites—African Americans acknowledged and emphasized the communities populating those wild places.[4]

The wilderness was a place to roam and hide for a moment's peace from slaveholders, or it could be a means of permanent escape. It was also a source of both sustenance and healing as slaves hunted animals and gathered medicinal plants. The woods and swamps were also dangerous, not only because of predatory animals but also because of predatory whites who used dogs to track runaways from the plantations and farms. Wilderness could be a haven or a nightmare for blacks. These positive and negative forces made the wild theirs, for better or worse, even though, in contrast to many whites, most African Americans did not legally own the soil or a single tree or twig.

African Americans characterized the soil or land in their own way. Though they cultivated Southern land, they did not express a sense of entitlement or ownership over it, nor did they generally subscribe to the white notion of land "belonging" to people. As the ruling class in a racially defined society, whites defined land ownership as traced from their European origins, which continued when they claimed Plymouth Rock and the rest of a land that was already populated by Native Americans. This sense of entitlement was reinforced with ownership of farms and plantations.

By contrast, African Americans rarely were able to lay consistent claim to any property. Those who did not meet white criteria for legal ownership of land did lay claim to cultivated places, but this claim had to be defined differently from that of whites. When African Americans worked someone else's land, they took some pride in their crops if not the land. In addition, if their ancestors were buried on property that was owned by whites, that land remained a link to their ancestors, making the soil sacred to a mother, a father, a sister, a brother, a wife, or a husband. Such forms of identification and connectedness with the environment have been largely ignored by whites because they do not fit the white paradigm of land ownership or even their conceptualization of wilderness.

African Americans' understanding of wilderness and the land bagan to transform with their increasing assimilation into American culture and the apparent possibility of their owning more land after emancipation. The oppression of racism concerning land was double-edged. Segregation stripped African Americans of their human, social, and political rights but ironically reinforced traditions by keeping African Americans knitted together on segregated wild or cultivated Southern landscapes. Racism and segregation resulted in inequitable access to quality land, including agriculture and environmental amenities like parks for leisure and play. Such segregation still exists today, with the wealthiest people—more often than not, whites—enjoying access to private beaches and land.

Such acts of environmental racism—inequality in which people of color not only have less access to environmental amenities like parks and pools compared with whites but also are exposed to higher rates of environmental toxins—began with monoculture, a single crop such as cotton or tobacco grown on a large scale for profit. Racism fueled Southern monoculture and agriculture, giving legitimacy to slaveholders' exploitation of the skills and labor of the enslaved, who rapidly and extensively redefined the Southern landscape. The turpentine industry, for example, was powered by black peonage on the cusp of the twentieth century. African Americans were forced to live in tents and shanties in the woods, stripping trees and tapping turpentine and rosin, thereby enriching whites who kept African Americans in neobondage after the period of enslavement.

Long before the birth of the modern environmental movement, African Americans practiced environmentalism through the lenses of religion, agriculture, gardening, and nature study. These practices have been documented in Africa as well as during enslavement, through the twentieth century, and even today. Ultimately, African Americans constructed a scaffold from existing knowledge of the environment in the community, at times borrowing and refining preservation, conservation, and agricultural methods from many groups, including the government and African American schools and camps.

In an attempt to show the human side of preservation-conservation, I have fictional vignettes open each chapter. These stories reflect my own journey through much research and writing and feel, to some extent, like my own story.

The study of environmental history traditionally encompasses ecology, geography, and history. But throughout this book I challenge readers as I draw, too, on Africa and African art, literature, history, theology, and many other fields in the tradition of sociologist W. E. B. DuBois and historian Carter G. Woodson. In doing so, I hope to widen our perspective of what the environment means, or can mean, to the people who inhabit it.

This said, unearthing the letters and autobiographies cited in this book required the skills of a treasure hunter. This is because some whites generally deemed the papers too insignificant to save and collect through the mid–twentieth century. Further, documents were not written in great quantities because of illiteracy, particularly among the enslaved, domestics, and sharecroppers. As a result, giving voice to the African American experience has been a challenge that I have attempted to meet.

The resulting book is a quilt work designed from this detective's loving labor to reveal the thoughts of farmers, artists, and novelists dotted throughout the South. This book is about individual stories in the African diaspora. I am thankful I was able to give voice to a creative and evocative people. This book is a true labor of love, an homage to every and any person in the African diaspora who was a farmer or a dirt-eater, a woman who cradled a bouquet of flowers, or a child who wondered at the flight of a moth.

1

The Atlantic Ocean

CURRENTS OF LIFE AND DEATH

The ocean is calm as an aged woman sitting in the shade of her wraparound porch, then fearsome as a man with a gun battling in the trenches at war, and later truculent as a two-year-old child writhing on the floor demanding she have her way. Zeus, a young black boy enslaved in Alabama, knows the idiosyncrasies and uncertainties of seafaring life. In 1771 Matthew Samford gave his brother, Captain Marshall Samford, the seven-year-old Zeus, to the heartache of Zeus's parents, Joseph and Lois. To these white men, Zeus was just another enslaved child sold off or given away as a gift, simply chattel.

The boy begins his travels as a personal servant twenty miles north of Mobile, boarding the merchant ship *Pegasus*. At first, Zeus's duties are limited to tending to the needs of Captain Samford, who requires constant attention, including grooming, cleaning, and feeding. As the boy grows older, his duties shift to those of chief cook. He is fortunate in that, before he was given away, he had sat in the kitchen with his mother and picked up cooking skills, duties most often confined to women on farms and plantations. Only men compose the ship's crew, so Zeus's cooking skills are welcomed as he supervises the chief steward and steward's assistant in the galley.

Blacks are often limited to cooking and cleaning on ships, but Zeus dreams of being one of the few blacks to captain his own ship, envisioning himself at the helm of a vessel cutting through the choppy waters of the Atlantic. He cooks in large pots over the stoves in the blistering galley in the Caribbean's tropical zone. Alternately, when the *Pegasus* sails through the cold, dark waters off the shores of England, he finds a bit of warmth by the stove. Thankfully the rolling waters do not trigger seasickness. Zeus stands on the deck in the worst weather with the wind driving rain into his chest. He sees spinner dolphins and humpback whales rising to the surface from the deep Caribbean waters and watches for hours the jumps, spins, flips, and turns of these sea creatures.

During his shore leaves in the Kingston harbor in Jamaica, Zeus wanders through the fishing shanties. The fishermen live on the edge of the harbor and walk quickly to their small boats, which are filled with nets and hooks. Wading on the beach, Zeus sees a two-foot parrot fish in the shoals, shallow sandbanks. Its mouth is white and black, and its upper body, from the dorsal and caudal fins down to the lateral line, is a brilliant blue; the remainder of the lower body to the pectoral and pelvic fins is yellow and red. Zeus also spends his downtime sleeping on the white sand, which is covered in seashells and skittering crabs. He sometimes finds extra work like caulking ships so he can earn money to purchase his freedom in the future.

For this one imagined tale there are many true maritime narratives by and histories of African Americans, such as that of Olaudah Equiano, who braved the Arctic, and Nancy Prince, a black woman who ventured to Russia and Jamaica. Other African American adventurers on the high seas include Harry Dean, James Forten, Paul Cuffee, John Jea, and William B. Gould. People of the African diaspora purposefully took to the Atlantic Ocean currents, including the North Equatorial and South Equatorial, on every manner of vessel from canoes to sloops, men-of-war, schooners, and whalers. According to the whims and desires of whites, others of the diaspora were also scattered across and tossed along the currents that drew ships to the Americas and Europe—all part of the Atlantic slave trade.

In *Black Jacks: African American Seamen in the Age of Sail*, W. Jeffrey Bolster argues that for many seafaring blacks, the ocean represented livelihood, empowerment, and identity, not enslavement and victimization. "An image of manacled ancestors crammed together aboard slave ships has triumphed as the association of African Americans and the sea," writes Bolster. This image of African Americans as victims rather than survivors with power is much different from the reality of black sailors during the Civil War who, Bolster argues, "were central to African Americans' collective sense of self, economic survival, and freedom struggle—indeed central to the very creation of black America." The legacy of black sailors persisted beyond the Civil War to the present: African Americans have continued their seafaring as part of the modern United States Navy.

The Atlantic slave trade from the late sixteenth to the mid–nineteenth century spanned the Middle Passage and the Civil War, with its naval battles during the age of sail, and ushered in a nascent maritime globalization through commercial, whaling, and military seafaring. Africans on commercial passenger and merchant ships dramatically and irrevocably expanded the boundaries and meaning of environment as they pushed off from African shores and stepped onto landscapes that were new to them in the Americas, the Caribbean, and Europe. Their travels on the Atlantic Ocean were complicated as they sought adventure, experienced oppression, and resisted subjugation.[1]

Seafaring supported a global economic system of mercantilism based on silver and gold bullion in exchange for American and European goods. The labor of enslaved Africans and African Americans supported this economic system into the nineteenth century. From this labor, whites cultivated cotton, tobacco, sugarcane, and indigo that they traded to Europeans. These goods were transported by ships on which blacks were free or enslaved crew members. Black sailors worked in an exploitative and racist economic system in which whites profited at the expense of others.

Seafaring blacks were at times victimized, but they also aimed to control their destinies. For example, they served as cultural conduits, traveling the oceans and connecting blacks to one another on land. London was the economic center of the Atlantic slave trade and the hub for information carried by word of mouth and through objects gathered by black seafaring people. Blacks used the ocean as a low-tech Internet of sorts to carry foreign goods and news, including the latest on the abolition movement.

Long before the age of sail, ancient Africans paddled and rowed small and large canoes and navigated their own ships on the waters, many of the latter fitted with sails. Africans arrived by ship in Central and South America, predating the Spanish and Portuguese invasion of the Americas and the Caribbean.

In the early fourteenth century, Abubakari II, a ruler of Mali, conferred with and was influenced by scholars at the University of Timbuktu who argued the world was round, countering medieval European scientists and philosophers, many of whom supported the world-is-flat theory. Ivan Van Sertima in *They Came Before Colum-*

bus: The African Presence in Ancient America says, "Water fascinated Abubakari the Second—spacious, mobile, brooding bodies of water. Water was like stored grain at Niani, for it took a full day for the servants to fill the royal jars in the river Kala and return with them to the palace."[2] The fruit of Abubakari's oceanic fascination was a fleet set to sail on the Atlantic Ocean into the unknown. Abubakari's foray speaks to how people, including Africans, were bound by a desire to find and explore new places. The ocean was the means of transport that often took center stage, though voyagers faced danger and perhaps death.

Abubakari sent four hundred ships to the coast from Mali, located in the interior of West Africa, via the Senegal River. They sailed westward, crossing the Atlantic for the Americas. It was a formidable passage, worsened since the final destination was Brazil, at a distance of more than four thousand miles.

Imagine these ships tossing in the churning waves, the rain coming down from above, blinding the Africans manning the sails. The women and children huddled together in the hold against the storms. Keep in mind that, according to Van Sertima, African "men were more terrified of the sea than the vast, blinding plains of the Sahara" and "the Arabs called the ocean 'the green sea of darkness'" as the Africans ventured forward with nothing but the horizon and water stretching ahead and behind. One captain returned to Mali, frightened when the fleet was hit by a storm. The rest of the fleet might have survived and sailed farther, on to South America after braving the storm.[3]

Such a setback did not dull the lure of the sea for Abubakari, who continued to gaze westward across the land of Mali to the Atlantic Ocean and the nameless places beyond. He organized a second fleet that he led himself, leaving his brother to rule Mali. As had been true of the last voyage, some of the ships were filled with cargo— enough food and water for shiploads of people on a long journey.

Abubakari never returned to Mali, though griots still tell his story through oral traditions practiced today in Africa.

Both of Abubakari's fleets sailed the North Equatorial current, streams that flow clockwise, drawn by the earth's rotational pull, beginning in West Africa and ending in the Americas. Abubakari and the other sailors and passengers probably stepped onto the silvery white sands of Brazil. Some may have looked longingly back for a few moments at the azure blue water and the rough surf tinged white with foam, wondering about the rivers, fields, lakes, savannahs, and forests left behind in Africa. Ahead of them, though, was the edge of the vast Amazon basin. Who knows how many varieties of plants, mammals, amphibians, reptiles, and insects lived in the forests before so many species were eradicated through the twenty-first century?

The climate was tropical, ninety degrees Fahrenheit at its hottest, with drenching rain that turned to high humidity at the end of a shower or storm. In the Amazon, depending on how deep the explorers ventured in, they most likely saw rainforests, savannahs, and the massive Amazon River with its many tributaries threading even farther and wider into lakes, swamps, and bogs. The length has been measured at approximately four thousand miles but has varied, since rivers shift over time. They would have encountered an astounding biodiversity in the forests—a high of seventy degrees Fahrenheit under the canopy—that included mangrove, fig, palm, mahogany, and Brazil-nut trees. In the freshwaters of the basin were crocodiles, tree frogs, stingrays, and dolphins. Parrots, macaws, and monkeys populated the trees. Jaguars and anteaters moved on the ground beneath the understory of the Amazon forests. Lizards, snakes, katydids, grasshoppers, butterflies, and moths moved from the trees to the ground and back again.

Back in Africa, the ancients made short forays, paddling in canoes gutted and carved out of trees for fishing, exploring, and simply traveling in order to trade from the shores. From the sixteenth century, the origins of the Atlantic slave trade, free Africans working as middlemen used canoes to transport to European ships the "goods"— their fellow Africans—destined for trade in the Americas. In small vessels, the Africans expertly braved the shallow waters and swelling waves that Europeans could not navigate with large ships. Many different ethnic groups, from the Mandinka to the Ashanti, were forced on a frightening and mysterious voyage across the Atlantic Ocean to the Americas under the tyrannical control of whites, including the Portuguese and the British.[4]

An estimated twenty million Africans took countless one-way voyages via the Middle Passage, an arduous trip with health and environmental implications that severely rearranged and transformed their lives. Africans vomited because of the effects of the rolling ocean. They suffered—and many died from—the bloody flux, a gory diarrhea. The people were raped, contracting syphilis—at its worst, resulting in dementia and death—from the European sailors. As many as four hundred Africans were chained to one another, head to toe, in the hold of a ship in a suffocating space as high as a coffin and only as wide as a body length. Skittering and creeping about the closed, suffocating hold were vermin like roaches, lice, rats, and mice. Gruel was ladled out into grasping hands and stuffed into gaping mouths in the center of crazed, terrorized faces. The smell was a noxious jumble to the senses—rotted food, body odor, foul feces, ammonia-steeped urine, and congealed blood. The worst were the dead bodies decomposing in that organic stew for days before the whites removed them. Water was rationed and often ran out long before the ships landed in the Americas. Some of the few comforts, if madness had not taken over, were fresh ocean air, the spray of salt water, and glimpses from the deck of whales and dolphins breaking the surface of the water.

Some Africans documented their own Middle Passage journeys. Ayuba Suleiman Diallo came from a Senegambian family of Muslim clerics, all of whom were educated and literate in Arabic. Representing his father, Diallo met a British ship at the outlet of the Gambia River in West Africa to sell two enslaved Africans in 1730. Failing to make an exchange that benefited his father financially, Diallo moved on. Though admonished by his father not to do so, Diallo crossed the Gambia River—which served as a partition against the Mandingoes, an aggressive people—where he finally sold the Africans. Ultimately, Diallo himself, adorned in gold and defenseless, was an attractive target; he was captured and sold by the Mandingoes to the British, who were waiting where the Atlantic Ocean and the Gambia River met.

As a devout Muslim, Diallo prayed to God, or Allah, the requisite five times a day. His prayers may have also helped ease the emotional strain of being enslaved aboard the British ship *Arabella*— ironic since he had been selling enslaved people himself. Perhaps he prayed for protection from the crashing waves and churning waters surrounding the vessel. Thomas Bluett, an antislavery advocate and author of Diallo's memoir, traveled with Diallo, ensuring safe passage to England. Bluett wrote, "During the Voyage, he was very constant in his Devotions; which he never omitted, on any Pretense, notwithstanding we had exceeding bad Weather all the time we were at Sea."[5]

Diallo landed in Maryland, an alien landscape, and quickly charmed the whites around him with his education and knowledge of trade. As a result, they allowed him to contact his father to request money to be freed. Bluett later describes how Diallo, upon entering the English Channel, sought to fix his surroundings firmly in his mind for future use as a bridge between African and English culture:

> By his good Nature and Affability he gained the good Will
> of all the Sailors, who (not to mention other kind of Offices)

all the way up the Channel fhewed him the Head Lands and remarkable Places; the Names of which Job wrote down carefully, together with the Accounts that were given him about them. His Reafon for doing, he told me, was, that if he met with any *Englisfhman* in his Country, he might by their Marks be able to convince him that he had been in *England*.

Diallo might have believed that having knowledge or experience in common with the Europeans would protect him from enslavement in future encounters. In 1734, Diallo landed where he had begun, in Africa, after sailing the reverse Middle Passage—an exception rather than the rule for the millions of Africans stolen from Africa—returning to his homeland and father.[6]

Diallo calmly sought solace from God during his voyage, but Olaudah Equiano had a more mixed experience. Equiano was from Benin, also in West Africa, and was born in 1745. His memories of the Middle Passage from childhood were of being snatched and kidnapped from his home by other Africans and forced to cross the Atlantic Ocean. Equiano says, "One day, when we had a smooth sea and moderate wind, two of my wearied countrymen who were chained together (I was near them at the time), preferring death to such a life of misery, somehow made through the nettings and jumped into the sea."

Perhaps the fear of open water prevalent among contemporary African Americans has its origin in the Middle Passage, echoes of psychological terror and torture at the hands of whites. I remember when I worked at a university and a staff member was planning a trip for African American teens, to venture out by boat into the Louisiana marshes. He asked me to talk to a mother who refused to let her son out on the water. This was back in 2004 when many of the marshes were in such a state that it was like being out in open water in the Gulf of Mexico. My colleague became angry when I explained that I would not try to change the woman's mind because stories or phantoms of stories about seafaring terrors going back to the Middle Passage might have been handed down to her, causing her fear of open water.

One such seafaring terror was the closeness in the hold that, according to Equiano, "produced copious perspirations so that the air soon became unfit for respiration from a variety of loathsome smells, and brought sickness among the slaves, of which many died." The lack of ventilation and the heat were worsened by "the galling chains" and "the filth of the necessary tubs, into which children often fell and were almost suffocated."[7]

It is difficult to imagine anything lighthearted about such a harrowing trip. Equiano did find something, though—probably a catalyst into a life as a seaman. During his passage, Equiano, then a child, was allowed more freedom than the adults and spent much of his time on deck. There he saw flying fish, which he said "surprised me very much." With a sense of wonder Equiano says the fish "used frequently to fly across the ship and many of them fell on the deck." He was also exposed to a bit of navigation when he saw a quadrant used for navigating the ocean and was astounded that the tool could guide mariners from one point on the earth to another. The sailors allowed him to look through the nautical instrument: "The clouds appeared to me to be land, which disappeared as they passed along. This heightened my wonder, and I was now more persuaded than ever that I was in another world and that everything about me was magic."[8]

Equiano caught the maritime bug on his first voyage in this age of sail. Many other experiences as a seaman were to follow, including trips to the Caribbean and the Arctic. He described a spiritual moment when he survived a shipwreck in the Bahamas:

> By this time the surf was foaming round us and made a dreadful noise on the breakers, and the very moment we let the

anchor go the vessel struck against the rocks. One swell now succeeded another, as it were one wave calling on its fellow: the roaring billows increased, and with one single heave of the swells the sloop was pierced and transfixed among the rocks! In a moment a scene of horror presented itself to my mind such as I never had conceived or experienced before. All my sins stared me in the face, and especially I thought that God had hurled his direful vengeance on my guilty head for cursing the vessel on which my life depended.[9]

Proselytized by whites who acculturated and assimilated Africans into European and American culture, Equiano converted to Christianity, a change of heart that became apparent when he recognized his sins in the midst of danger.

The legal standing of blacks on the ocean versus land could mean the difference between justice and inequity, freedom and enslavement. Equiano described an interracial marriage in St. Kitts.

A white man wanted to marry in the church a free black woman that had land and slaves in Montserrat, but the clergyman told him it was against the law of the place to marry a white and a black in church. The man then asked to be married on the water, to which the parson consented, and the two lovers went in one boat and the parson and clerk in another, and thus the ceremony was performed.[10]

Nancy Prince's experience was a more personal one. An African American woman with roots in Massachusetts, she grew up during the nineteenth century in a family of seamen, including her father, stepfather, and brother. Prince must have learned by listening to and observing her relatives. Leaving Jamaica for the second time, she proved her knowledge of navigation by warning the passengers that "the vessel was tacked to a south-west course" when in fact they should have been headed to the northeastern coast of the United States. The captain's plan was to sell off the blacks on the vessel at Key West, Florida. Prince knew the law and refused to step onto land, knowing she could be enslaved. The captain attempted the same ploy in the New Orleans harbor. According to Prince, "Every inducement was made to persuade me to go ashore."[11] Whites in the South did not even need the Fugitive Slave Acts of 1793 and 1850, which allowed whites to capture runaways and enslave free blacks in the United States, since blacks had little legal recourse. Stepping onto Louisiana soil would mean immediate enslavement for Prince.

Both the marriage between a white man and black woman described by Equiano and Nancy Prince's struggle to remain free involved the confluence of land, law, and inequity. Land often meant ownership for whites, but for people of African descent, land placed limits on freedom and reinforced enslavement. In these instances, the ocean was a safer place.

Harry Dean descended from a family of seamen, including Paul Cuffee, who ran his trading ships past the British blockade during the American Revolution. Dean was also the captain of the *Pedro Gorino*, a commercial ship. He was born in 1864 and was fifty when his autobiography was published in 1929. When he was twelve years old, Dean visited Atlantic City with his family; this trip provided one of the first indications that he had a true connection with the ocean. Dean says he "swam in the sea and played on the beaches in the sunshine." He adds, "Suddenly I was crazy for the sea. The salty tang in the air, rough sailors, the glamour about boats, the stories of adventure I had heard all through my childhood, filled me with a tremendous urge."

While still a child, Dean traveled on a merchant ship with his uncle. In the Gulf of Mexico, Dean says, "the weather was clear," "the water was as blue as indigo, shading to green," and "the sky curved over us like a silver bell." He adds, "When I went on deck each morning I could hardly believe my senses." Dean offered similar vivid images of the ocean throughout his autobiography, reflecting a genuine love and awe for the ocean.[12]

Frederick Douglass, who lived from 1818 to 1895, was a more famous contemporary of Harry Dean and Nancy Prince. Though once enslaved, he was later freed and became a leading abolitionist. He moved around quite a bit in Maryland but at one point lived a short distance from the Chesapeake Bay. He described the region,

> whose broad bosom was ever white with sails from every quarter of the habitable globe. The beautiful vessels, robed in purest white, so delightful to the eye of the freeman, were to me so shrouded as ghosts, to terrify and torment me with thoughts of my wretched condition. I have often, in the deep stillness of a summer's Sabbath, stood all alone upon the lofty banks of that noble bay, and traced with saddened heart and tearful eye, the countless number of sails moving off the might ocean.[13]

Douglass gave nature human attributes, describing the bay as noble and the ocean as mighty. The ocean also signified freedom for him.

I often feel that awe myself when I go to the ocean. I once lived in Playa del Rey, California, not far from Venice Beach, and I remember watching a seal sunning on the beach and surfers becoming one with the water.

The stories told above, including Douglass's maritime experiences, took place on the Atlantic Ocean and focus on merchant seaman, leaving much to be explored. Blacks also traveled the Indian and Arctic Oceans and the Mediterranean Sea. They were pirates, whalers, and naval sailors. The Atlantic Ocean routes also served as foodways by which seeds and crops were transported, changing the agricultural practices and landscapes on the other side of the Atlantic, miles from Africa. Africans cultivated gourds, beans, and cotton that were introduced purposefully or by accident in the Americas.

The contemporary novelist Charles Johnson's rendering of the sea in *Middle Passage* (1998) speaks to the primacy of life aboard ship—what might have been. In the early stages of the novel, Johnson sets a tableau of the beautiful sea that, like God, is the creation of all things. Like the protagonist, Rutherford Calhoun, a sailor or even a pirate might have thought longingly and lovingly of the sea. Calhoun says,

> Wind off the water was like a fist of fresh air, a cleansing blow that made me feel momentarily clean. In the spill of yellow moonlight, I'd shuck off my boots and sink both feet into the water. But the pier was most beautiful, I think, in early morning, when sunlight struck the wood and made it steam as moisture and mist from the night before evaporated. Then you could believe, like the ancient philosopher Thales, that the analogue for life was water, the formless omnific sea.[14]

Similarly Suleiman, Equiano, Prince, Dean, and Douglass had visions and an intimate understanding of the Atlantic Ocean. What else does the historical record hold? The answer can be found in nature. As Bolster writes, "As winds and currents kept the ocean itself from stasis, so seafaring men of color stirred black society and shaped Atlantic maritime culture."[15]

Today the legacy of these seafaring adventurers is largely obscured. Many African Americans stay away from nature, including the water. Some of the residual stories of the Middle Passage remain part of African American lore, however transformed and distant from enslavement African Americans may be today.

Rue Mapp, founder of Outdoor Afro, speaks to such residual terror as she relates the experience of snorkeling with other African Americans on a vacation in St. Croix:

> [Their] expressions of alarm felt more like a visceral terror that echoed from a past coded in our DNA. In that instant, I considered the Middle Passage, which incidentally trudged over those same Caribbean waters, and in that fleeting moment, remembering the narrative of our past, the panic of my travel mates seemed justified.[16]

Blacks stay away from water for other reasons, too. Some African American women avoid swimming and water sports because it takes so much time and money to do their hair, or because when they do go in the water with their hair in its natural state, without weaves, they are embarrassed about how it looks wet. Such practical considerations lead to less time in nature. This is a shame, since nature, including swimming in our oceans and lakes, feeds the soul.

2

Topography

NAVIGATING THE SOUTHERN LANDSCAPE

Jena—Joseph and Lois's daughter—was sold off the Samford plantation north of Mobile, Alabama, when she was just twelve years old. Her lot became even harder than what she had experienced in Alabama when she was moved once again off the coast of Georgia. Jena, now a nineteen-year-old woman, looks out at the rain, a drizzle edging toward a torrent. She stands at the threshold of the cabin in the slave quarters, knowing that, rain or shine, she will be forced to go to the fields to protect the slaveholder's rice against flooding after several days of heavy rain.

Jena learned to cultivate rice from the descendents of Africans who had also cared for her when she was sold away. She steps out, and her thin shift quickly clings to her sunburned skin as she walks along a stony, hilly path past the loblolly pine she often leans against in brief and solitary respites. Jena limps—the result of a lingering injury from when the slaveholder knocked her down a year ago—toward the rice fields with several others. They are met by the overseer, who appears sour about the weather and the slow progress of work. She looks to the pond, illuminated by a jagged line of lightning, that feeds water to the fields where she spends days cultivating rice with her feet planted in wet soil and at times hip-deep in water. Connected and farther on are the saltwater marshes and beyond those the Atlantic Ocean. Jena considers escaping on a ship headed north to the Philadelphia port, though she fears the open water. Suddenly she feels the lash across her shoulders, wrapping around low to her abdomen and painfully ending her reverie. After stumbling from the lash, Jena grudgingly turns back to the fields to reinforce the banks, dikes, and floodgates as she thinks again about running from the slaveholder's fists and the overseer's lash to freedom.

A fricans and African Americans had varied and often invisible perceptions of the environment, as glimpsed through this woman's illusory moments in Georgia, working and living on the land. Exploring such perceptions debunks the myth of the African American antienvironmentalist and underscores the fact that African Americans perceived wilderness and the land in distinctive ways. While the environmental histories of African Americans are defined by many viewpoints and locales, the ways in which blacks navigated the geographical swath of the American South can serve as broad, general context.

Enslaved and later free Africans and African Americans lived and worked on several distinctive land formations or bands. These formations run from north to south and parallel to one another. Starting from the Atlantic Ocean and moving westward to the Mississippi River, the major regions are the Coastal Plain; the Piedmont; the

Appalachians, including the Blue Ridge, the Ridge and Valley, and the Appalachian Plateau; and the Alluvial Lowlands. The Coastal Plain extends approximately three thousand miles from the Atlantic to the Gulf Coast, its width varying from less than a mile to five hundred miles. Lagoons, beaches, swamps, savannahs, and offshore islands dot the coastline. Just to the west, the Fall Line divides the Coastal Plain and the Piedmont, stretching approximately 900 miles from New York to Alabama, with widths up to 125 miles. This terrain is marked by deep, narrow streams and valleys.[1]

The Appalachians include the Blue Ridge Mountains, Ridge and Valley Mountains, and Appalachian Plateau. The Blue Ridge, the loftiest of the Appalachian mountain ranges, interspersed with valleys, creates a scenic tableau with the highest peaks rising to three thousand feet. The Ridge and Valley, where flat, fertile valleys sit among sharp, straight ridges, are distinctive from the Piedmont and Blue Ridge. The Appalachian Plateau, a hilly expanse "with narrow, winding valleys and uplands mantled with thin, poor soil" blankets parts of West Virginia, Kentucky, Tennessee, and northern Alabama.

African Americans' resistance to slavery transformed the meaning of this Southern topography covered and shaped by water, woods, soil, and weather. The landscape described here in rough strokes was negotiated, whether in people's imaginations or in reality, during enslavement and continuing into freedom. This is true in Frederick Douglass's *Narrative of the Life of Frederick Douglass, an American Slave* (1845), a narrative and an autobiography, and W. E. B. DuBois's *The Souls of Black Folk* (1903), a social commentary and collection of his own essays. Though the men were from mid-Atlantic and Northern states, respectively, their works offer insight into runaways' experiences in the South.

As a young enslaved man, Douglass concocted but did not carry out a plan to run away with a small band of four other enslaved men in Maryland. The state, while not quite the South, was still emblematic of the enslaved runaway's experience. Douglass writes of this imagined escape:

> On one hand, there stood slavery, a stern reality, glaring frightfully upon us,—its robes already crimsoned with the blood of millions, and even now feasting itself greedily upon our own flesh. On the other hand, away back in the dim distance, under the flickering light of the north star, behind some craggy hill or snow-covered mountain, stood a doubtful freedom—half frozen—beckoning us to come and share its hospitality.

The nightmarish flight continues as Douglass and the other runaways are confounded by human barriers, ford a river, and enter woods that prove sinister. He imagines, "At every gate through which we were to pass, we saw a watchman—at every ferry a guard—on every bridge a sentinel—and in every wood a patrol." He shifts from the woods and river to the ocean—where he and the others would make their way north to freedom. Then they are back to the woods, where the tracker's dogs enter the account. Scorpions, which could only be found in deserts and not Maryland woods, make an appearance, and finally Douglass's invented tableau transitions to rivers, wild beasts, and woods:

> Now we were contending with the waves, and were drowned; now we were overtaken, and torn to pieces by the fangs of the terrible bloodhound. We were stung by scorpions, chased by wild beasts, bitten by snakes, and finally after having nearly reached the desired spot,—after swimming rivers, encountering wild beasts, sleeping in the woods, suffering hunger and nakedness,—we were overtaken by our pursuers, and, in our resistance, we were shot dead on the spot!

With this vengeful hunt for runaways through woods populated by a hound and whites and more whimsically but dangerously crawling with scorpions, Douglass imagines landscapes to be escaped and potential paths to freedom from enslavement that are neither worshipful nor adoring of nature. Ultimately, the runaways plan to take a canoe on the Chesapeake Bay, "a distance seventy or eighty miles from where we lived." Although their conspiracy to flee enslavement never transpired, this account makes clear that the woods and swamps were fearsome places populated by even more fearsome whites and not tranquil retreats akin to the idyllic refuge later described in Henry David Thoreau's *Walden*.[2] African Americans did not "find themselves" in the wilderness; instead they found, potentially, deliverance from lives of servitude.

Much like Douglass, DuBois—an elite Northern African American who lived in the South for a time—set resistance against the backdrop of nature in the swamp and forests of Dougherty County, Georgia, also called the Egypt of the Confederacy, in the black belt. In a lyrical way, he describes the frontier that began in part in the Southeast during the colonial period:

> First there is the Swamp, to the west, where the Chickasaw-hatchee flows sullenly southward. The shadow of an old plantation lies at its edge, forlorn and dark. Then comes the pool; pendent gray moss and brackish waters appear, and forests filled with wildfowl. In one place the wood is on fire, smoldering [sic] in dull red anger; but nobody minds. Then the swamp grows beautiful; a raised road, built by chained Negro convicts, dips down into it, and forms a way walled and almost covered in living green. Spreading trees spring from a prodigal luxuriance of undergrowth; great dark green shadows fade into the black background, until all is one mass of tangled semi-trop-

ical foliage, marvelous in its weird savage splendor. Once we crossed a black silent stream, where the sad trees and writhing creepers, all glinting fiery yellow and green, seemed like some vast cathedral,—some green Milan builded of wildwood.

DuBois reaches back seventy years from Georgia to Florida and back to Georgia again after outlining the contours of the swamp filled with trees. He continues, "Osceola, the Indian-Negro chieftain, had risen in the swamps of Florida, vowing vengeance. His war-cry reached the red creeks of Dougherty, and his war-cry ran from the Chattahoochee to the sea." The conquered chief becomes the conqueror:

Men and women and children fled and fell before them as they swept into Dougherty. . . . Then the false slime [of the swamp] closing about them called white men from the east. Waist-deep, they fought beneath the tall trees, until the war-cry was hushed and the Indians glided back into the west. Small wonder the wood is red.[3]

For this "Indian-Negro" and even DuBois, wilderness was weighted with social meaning, a place that was painfully negotiated rather than the environmental paradise often depicted by whites.

Blacks and whites experienced the weather and climate of the South differently too. Weather varies throughout the South, from hot summers to freezing winters. Farthest south, in states such as Florida, the weather is subtropical, with shorts and T-shirts the norm. But even in areas of the Deep South there are periods of freezing temperatures that result in snow sticking to the grass and ice coating the ground.

These variations contribute to a distinctively Southern relationship between culture and environment. In *Climate and Southern Dis-*

tinctiveness, A. Cash Koeniger asserts, "The question is not whether the South has had a warm environment, compounded by humidity, but whether the effect of that environment on southern behavioral patterns and history has been significant." Certainly, this was true for Africans, whose labor often revolved around the changing weather and climate patterns. Koeniger points out that the enslaved were attentive not just to expected rain, floods, and other phenomena but also to "changes in the phases of the moon, to animal behavior and plant growth patterns that were 'signs' of weather change, [and] to variations of light and cloud patterns"[4]

Weather often defined African Americans' experiences with nature, whether they were enslaved or free. Whites' control of the social, economic, and political lives of blacks framed how blacks traversed and worked in the Southern climate. Fannie Berry of St. Petersburg, Virginia, recalled a harrowing instance of racism when she labored for the "marse" as a child while battered by the rain. The day was whiskey and rain soaked, with sinister implications, and the enslaved children were viewed and treated as subhuman, in effect as animals:

> One day a storm was comin' up and marster sen' me five miles to get him a drink of whiskey from missus' father's house—'member, missus' daddy 'stilled whiskey. When I go dar it was pouring rain. Well, ol' marse poured dis tickler full fer my young marster and sed, "Run along gal." Child, it poured, I mean, an' I didn't have on but one piece. I didn't know what to do so I took off dat and hung it 'cross my shoulders an' kep goin'. Water came up to my waist in ditches and placed in de road.[5]

Would a slaveholder have exposed his own small white child to the elements in this way? Berry's value was in her labor, so her drowning in a hard rain would have been a financial and not an emotional loss for this slaveholder.

None too distant in time from Berry's experiences, Ned Cobb, the Alabama sharecropper one or two generations removed from enslavement, also lived with the vagaries of weather during planting and harvesting in turn-of-the-twentieth-century Alabama. Rural African Americans like Cobb were consumed with shifting weather. A flood could inundate a tobacco field, and a heat wave could burn cotton down to dry, useless stalks. The tenuous nature of their lives was only exacerbated by the strained and violent racial climate of the period.[6]

Cobb had more autonomy than a small enslaved child inundated by a rainstorm, yet he was still trapped by the lingering effects of enslavement while he labored as a tenant. Thus he waited on good weather to plant his cotton: "If the weather's just right, you can plant the first days of the week and by the middle of the next week, you got a pretty stand of cotton all over your field." He waited on the cold to chop the crop: "Just as soon as that cotton gets up to a stand, best time to chop it out provided you feel that the cold won't get what you leave there. . . . If you chop it too early, decidin' wrong about what the weather's going to do, you go out there and thin out your crop, that bad weather come and get the balance of it." He waited on dry and wet spells: "Dry weather can cut the growth of that cotton to an extent. Too much rain can cause it to overgrow itself. Cotton's a sun weed. Too much water and it'll grow too fast." And finally, he waited on the sunlight, as the cotton budded:

> And that cotton turned yellow as a fox and shredded off every leaf on it, but left the buds. I examined it and it looked terrible—in a day or two when the weather moderated, I examined my little old cotton and seed it was still alive, and them buds, after the sun hit em good, turnin hot after the snap of

weather, little old cotton buds just kept livin and commenced
a puttin out.

For Cobb, the relationship between his culture and the South
defined his relationship with the environment. He struggled over
his desire to go to school versus the duties of tilling the land. As a
child, Cobb spoke his own truth—one of many African American
voices—concerning the fields, swamps, and woods. African American tenants and even farm owner-operators often sent their children
to the fields because they had no choice; farming required many
hands and left little or no time for education. Cobb was no different,
although Hayes, Cobb's father, was unusually cruel. While Hayes
hunted and fished for turkeys, ducks, and fish in the woods and
swamps—sources of sustenance and an outlet for leisure—he forced
nine-year-old Cobb to plow the fields alone as gnats nipped the boy's
tender flesh. Worse yet, Hayes whipped the boy for fighting off the
gnats and for his ragged plowing style. Though heat and humidity
were a given, Cobb does not mention either as he describes plowing
in the fields while his father hunted in the swamps.[7]

Cobb's responsibilities in the fields made it impossible for him
to attend school, though he envied how Hayes's mistress sent Wil-
lie, Cobb's half brother, to class consistently enough for him to learn
to read and write. Cobb remarks, "She sendin' my daddy's child to
school while he had me hard laboring all the time. I didn't never get
out of the first reader; got no education to speak of."[8] Though Cobb
desired an education, he was never able to transcend the harshness
of his rural experiences, which often required children, including
black children, to work.

Nature was tangled up with Cobb's and other rural African
Americans' thorny experiences. Even when Africans came to North
America, they did not lose their spiritual connection to animals,

trees, and the land. In Cobb's case, it is difficult to untangle what is African culture and what is Southern culture.

Surely some rural African Americans who survived enslavement looked to a cooling sunset, a wheeling bird, and a hard rain. Yet they inevitably turned their eyes, hands, and feet to the fields. With somewhat different sensibilities, African American farmers warily monitored the weather, the boll weevil, and the threat of floods—attempts to control and predict nature in order to succeed and survive. They perpetually bent, shaped, and twisted nature, etching out the Southern agroecosystem, a cash monoculture system of cotton, indigo, sugarcane, and tobacco crops.

In seemingly human ways, nature toyed with the farmers' precisely planted rows of cotton in exhausted soil, a feast for pests like the boll weevil. The impact on farmers was profound, with their sense of identity tied to productivity, which fluctuated with the droughts that dried cotton plants or the heavy rains that flattened crops and led to fungus, turning tobacco to rot. Farmers relied on timing and luck as they tried to outwit nature. Sadly many gave up on farming when their crops failed them one too many times. Yet other African American farmers struggled, survived, and were redeemed in the sunshine and rain, in valleys and atop hills, among pine and apple trees, and on rivers and lakes—all the backdrop—no, truly the foundation—of African American rural life.[9]

Southern agriculture was sustained by the soil and of course by the hands of African Americans like Berry and Cobb. Soils ranged from poor and sandy in the Coastal Plain to rich and alluvial in the Mississippi River Basin. High rainfall caused leaching and water runoff, which quickly made poor Southern soils less fertile. In addition, humidity and high temperatures produced rapid decomposition, resulting in soil leached of humus or organic content. In the Coastal Plain, soils were primarily sandy, suitable only for pine barrens, and contained fine silt, gravel, and clay, all lacking organic matter. The alluvial soils of the Mississippi Valley were fertile and supported cash crops like cotton. The Appalachians were generally rocky, consisting of quartz, sandstone, conglomerate, shale, and limestone.

The land, the soil, was a commodity or resource that many, both African Americans and whites, desired to control, particularly since more often than not it was owned by whites and worked by enslaved people and sharecroppers. Two literary characters, an African American couple in DuBois's *The Quest of the Silver Fleece* (1911), a novel of neoenslavement set in the Alabama woods and swamps, made claim to the land. In one scene, DuBois describes the soil, giving it human characteristics:

> Far away the wide black land that belts the South, where Miss Smith worked and Miss Taylor drudged and Bles and Zora dreamed, the dense black land sensed the cry and heard the bound of answering life within the vast dark breast. All that dark earth heaved in mighty travail with the bursting bolls of the cotton while black attendant earth spirits swarmed above sweating and crooning to its birth pains.

Bles and Zora, an African American couple, toiled on the land:

> The soil was virgin and black, thickly covered over with a tangle of bushes, vines, and smaller growth all brilliant with early leaves and wild flowers. "A pretty tough proposition for clearing and ploughing," said Bles, with practiced eye. But Zora eagerly surveyed the prospect. "It's where the Dreams lives," she whispered.[10]

Like a girl, the soil was virgin; like a man it had a breast; and like an old prophet it dreamed as Bles and Zora struggled to cultivate their own land.

Booker T. Washington deemed the soil to be a saving grace and fervently argued its benefits to African Americans. The famous president of Tuskegee Institute in Alabama, one of the first schools to provide education for African Americans, Washington was arguably the reigning African American leader in the South during the turn of the twentieth century and DuBois' archrival. He related a story in which a Tuskegee graduate had produced 266 bushels of sweet potatoes from just one acre on which only 49 bushels had normally been cultivated in the past. Washington touted the graduate's "knowledge of soil chemistry" and "improved methods of agriculture." Referring to African Americans, he bemoaned,

> How many times I wished then, and have often wished since, that by some magic power I might remove the great bulk of these people into the country districts and plant them upon the soil, upon the solid and never deceptive foundation of Mother Nature, where all nations and races that have ever succeeded have gotten their start—a start that at first may be slow and toilsome but one that is nevertheless real.[11]

Washington proclaimed the science of soil, while using the metaphor of "planting" African Americans like tobacco or corn as a rhetorical means of binding farmers to the rural South, where they would sustain agriculture, the Southern economy, and a rural way of life. In his own manner Washington tried to serve his people, while confined by the dictates of whites who wished to ensure that African Americans continued to farm. Migration to Southern and Northern cities by sharecroppers threatened white landowners, a problem Washington served to alleviate through his leadership of Tuskegee Institute, which provided agricultural education and training for African Americans. Education and job opportunities in farming kept black labor in the South.

Forests planted in this soil varied from region to region. Pine stretched from New Jersey to Texas, with longleaf pine best suited to the poor sandy soils of the Coastal Plain. Adjacent to the oak-chestnut forest, several species of pine, including loblolly and pitch, mixed with hardwoods in the Appalachians. Red maple, black locust, and sassafras struggled in the understory of the pine and oak. Oak, hickory, and pine barrens covered the Mississippi Valley, along with willows and cottonwoods bordering the rivers' shorelines and favoring low-lying, ill-drained areas.[12]

Trees had multiple meanings in African American culture; perhaps these meanings were an inheritance from Africa, though similar meanings are common in cultures across the globe. Slaves gave trees human attributes such as holiness or evilness and named them after people. Two African Americans—Clara Cotton McCoy and Booker T. Washington—responded to trees in their own ways, the former joyfully and the latter fearfully. McCoy, a slave in North Carolina, reminisced about apple trees blooming: "De blooms looked just like droves of pink butterflies flyin' on de sky." In contrast, when Washington was young and enslaved, he rode to a mill on a horse loaded with corn. After having the corn ground, he had an encounter with nature on the return trip home, perhaps in the dark, that tested him: "The road was a lonely one and often led through dense forests. I was afraid."[13]

Is it any wonder an enslaved child like Washington viewed the woods as a chilling, frightening place, given that this was where runaways were often captured, bitten by the dogs, tortured, and ultimately returned to slaveholders or shackled and sold off for disobedience to new places and owners?

As many Africans Americans have eloquently shown here, Southern wilderness had to be negotiated by the enslaved rather than possessed and conquered by them, in contrast to the experiences of many whites. Enslaved people were forced to treat nature as a source of clandestine escape routes, making their experiences in the woods so different from that of whites. In the South, from enslavement into the twentieth century, the land was generally owned by whites but worked by African Americans. This changed fields from places that were sources of hope and perhaps prosperity where crops were harvested to landscapes that simply meant hard, unremunerated work and excessive, brutal punishment suffered while doing that work.

Through these many perspectives, African Americans navigated the Southern landscape—mountains, weather, soils, forests, lakes, rivers, and an ocean. They defined their relationships with the environment through their own sense of community and living with the challenges of racist Southern society. All this made their experiences unique from those of whites and arguably had a profound impact on the environmental perceptions and attitudes of future generations.

3

Religion

SHOUTING IN THE WOODS

_____

The gatekeeper is Minkah, a young man a few years beyond his initiation into manhood. He stands with his head wrapped and body draped in white before the entrance to his village's earth shrine in the yellow-white afternoon sun in Ghana. He guards a place of worship where community members offer animal sacrifices to increase soil fertility, allocate land to members of the village, ceremoniously bury their dead, and venerate their ancestors—all practices with many variations throughout West Africa. Men from a neighboring village capture Minkah, battering him on the head and shoulders and then enveloping him in a net. The kidnappers drag him to British seamen waiting on the edge of Minkah's receding world, the western shores of Africa. After being imprisoned for two days, Minkah is shoved into the dim hold of a ship filled with Africans of diverse cultures and religious beliefs, bodies pressed together, shackled head to toe. Once free in Africa, "seasoned" in Jamaica, and now enslaved in Alabama, the gatekeeper is forced to adopt and later embraces a new religion, blending African spirituality with the Protestantism of the enslavers.

———————————————————————————————

Africans carried their religious experiences with nature to the New World through the onerous Middle Passage and colonial and antebellum enslavement, which transformed them. Although most African Americans had few or no direct ties with Africa during these periods, they retained African influences and straddled two cultures—one African and the other American—resulting in the transformation of African environmental spirituality.

African spirituality formed a backdrop to the African American experience. Africans, singly or in combination, based their spirituality on higher powers and a distant spiritual world, including the belief in a single God and lesser divinities, veneration of one's ancestors, and belief in supernatural events—generalizations that varied from village to village, region to region, and nation to nation. Broadly speaking, Africans believed in the interconnectedness of the human, spiritual, and environmental realms and felt that harm toward or care for one necessarily affected the others. For African farmers, the cycles of planting and harvesting, alpha and omega, and life and death were fundamental to nature and agriculture. Farmers consecrated and benefited from the soil, which was, in turn, a source of spirituality, nourishment, and life to humans. A seed that sprouted from the soil of a sacrosanct field was a metaphor for the circle of life and death, a touchstone in farming.

Africans blended the sublime with the commonplace, honoring the dead with ceremonial burials while returning nutrients to the soil. The Dogon, an ancient culture in Mali, West Africa, believed that the original farmers came "from the bowels of the earth," an apropos depiction and mythology of the origins of life for a people who tilled the soil. Other ethnic groups—the Ashanti of Ghana, the Mossi of Burkina Faso, and the Bambara of Sudan—honored nature by pouring mixtures of millet flour, water, and the blood of sacrificed chickens onto the corners of uncultivated fields, creating offerings, or shrines of a sort, by simultaneously consecrating the soil for planting and venerating their ancestors.[1]

In the United States, enslaved and, later, free people of African descent retained Africanisms in cuisine, marriage, family values, and expressive culture. Enslaved people experienced and understood the landscape through a worldview that ordered nature, combined spirituality and everyday life, and incorporated the animate and the inanimate. African religious influences were evident in dance (the ring shout), music (spirituals and gospel music), prayer (fervent expressions to God), and preaching (call-and-response between the pastor and congregation) and were ritualized in sacred groves or woods, the church, and daily life. Many of these influences have continued. In early twentieth-century Florida, African-born parents and grandparents modeled and taught "ritualized spiritual possession" to their young, and ministers' melodious preaching along with the spirit-filled moaning and cadences of choirs and congregations fill African American churches today. Novelist, essayist, and anthropologist Zora Neale Hurston wrote in the 1930s about the vestiges of Africanisms in the shout:

> There can be little doubt that shouting is a survival of the African "possession" of the Gods. In Africa it is sacred to the priesthood or acolytes; in America it has become generalized. The implication is the same, however; it is a sign of special favor from the spirit that it chooses to drive out the individual consciousness temporarily and use the body for its expression.[2]

Protestantism transformed the meaning of nature for African Americans as the black masses began to look to their ministers to interpret the Bible from the pulpit. Some laypeople, often illiterate, including the enslaved, took the initiative to blend formal church teachings with their own biblical interpretations of nature.[2]

Harriet Jacobs, a runaway who had been enslaved and went on to publish her memoir, *Incidents in the Life of a Slave Girl* (1861), typified how African Americans blended their distinctive spirituality and nature. Jacobs spent contemplative moments in a wooded church and graveyard. After gathering her children, who were to be christened at church, she was overwhelmed by her ancestral past: "When I entered the church, recollections of my mother came over me, and I felt subdued in spirit." Later, she stepped through the doors of the church:

> The graveyard was in the woods, and twilight was coming on. Nothing broke the death-like stillness except the occasional twitter of a bird. My spirit was overawed by the solemnity of the scene. For more than ten years I had frequented this spot, but never had it seemed to me so sacred as now. A black stump, at the head of my mother's grave, was all that remained of a tree my father had planted. His grave was marked by a small wooden board, bearing his name, the letters of which were nearly obliterated. I knelt down and kissed them, and poured forth a prayer to God for guidance and support in the perilous step I was about to take. As I passed the wreck of the old meeting house, where, before Nat Turner's time, the slaves had been allowed to meet for worship, I seemed to hear my father's voice come from it, bidding me not tarry till I reached freedom or the grave. I rushed on with renovated hopes. My trust in God had been strengthened by that prayer among the graves.

Intuitively Jacobs felt that she stood on hallowed ground and invoked the spirits of her parents along with the enslaved insurrectionist Nat Turner. She did this in a natural setting, in the woods at twilight, accompanied by a singing bird and a long-dead tree. The scene evokes African influences, including the planting of trees at graves, which symbolized an ancestral connection and the rising to heaven. At the same time, Jacobs looked to the Protestant God for direction as she prepared to flee Southern soil for freedom in the North.[3]

African Americans' religious beliefs concerning nature continued into the early twentieth century and were sometimes expressed through art. Clementine Hunter, born in 1886, was an African American folk artist from rural northwest Louisiana. Her paintings represent the beauty and shade of trees along with the practicality of soil, so essential to the farmer's livelihood. Hunter interpreted life and death in *Baptism* (circa 1950), an oil painting of a water baptism beside a rural church that exhibits African American and Protestant influences.

As a young woman Hunter witnessed plantation workers being baptized in the Cane River south of Natchitoches, the newly initiated believers affirming their faith according to the tenets of the Bible.[4] Her rendering of the African American church's baptism ritual, probably one of her first paintings, depicts a pastor, perhaps an elder, church members, and those waiting to be baptized—men in black and women in white—gathered near a whitewashed church close to the river.

Baptism evokes the rhythms of humanity and nature and draws on the duality of African American culture. From a Protestant perspective, Hunter borrowed the New Testament template of the water baptism ritual—in which one's old self dies and is "born again" in Christ—first performed by John the Baptist. This prophet, according to the Bible, "did baptize in the wilderness and preach the baptism of repentance for the remission of sins. And there went out unto him all the land of Judea, and they of Jerusalem, and were all baptized of him in the river of Jordan, confessing their sins." In Hunter's rendering, the old sinful selves die as the pastor submerges church members, revealing new women and men in Christ, who rise to the surface of the water against a tableau of trees, cotton, and grass. These various stages of life and death play out in *Baptism* on a fragment of Southern landscape defined by African American sharecroppers working for white landowners. Thus, Hunter transformed John the Baptist's New Testament wilderness bordering the River Jordan to an agrarian civilization of bottle-green grass, mauve skies, symmetrical, fanlike trees, and russet soil. All of these were well-known environmental markers of the daily lives of African Americans on the river, lives defined both by lingering African legacies and by the climate of racism that limited their experiences.[5]

Cane River, Hunter's home, was a fertile place for her art and for cotton cultivation during her adolescence and young adulthood. Her depiction of religious rites during this period of her life continued into her old age.

It is likely that both Jacobs and Hunter worshiped in the black Baptist or the African Methodist Episcopal (AME) churches, the leading Protestant denominations among African Americans from enslavement to the early twentieth century and following in popularity today behind the Pentecostal Church. Since the Baptist Church was the leading denomination among slaveholders, the same proved true for enslaved people, who attended segregated church services and organized secret worship and prayer meetings in the woods. The black Baptist Church grew slowly because slave codes prohibited large gatherings. George Liele founded the first African Baptist Church in Mecklenburg, Virginia, in 1758. The enslaved and later free people claimed the church as their own, with two distinctions from whites: the display of zeal or passion during church services and the informal entrée into the church of preachers and pastors with little or no formal education. From the late nineteenth century, the leadership and members organized Baptist conventions, significantly increasing the membership and expanding the church. Some African American leaders tried and failed to diminish the emotional emphasis of worship services, which appealed to a broader membership.[6]

In 1786, Richard Allen, once enslaved, purchased his own freedom and joined St. George's Methodist Episcopal Church in Philadelphia, a largely white congregation with some black members, both African and African American. A year later, during a church service, white members attacked black worshippers and dragged them from the altar. Such racism was typical of whites in the segregated Methodist Episcopal Church. As a result, Allen abandoned the experiment of a segregated church run by whites and became a pastor of the Bethel African Methodist Episcopal Church, where he was later ordained as a bishop in 1799.

In 1816, Allen's church merged with the AME Church, a national denomination consisting of local congregations with black membership. This was the first black denomination in the United States, selecting bishops to lead and monitor the churches, educating the formerly enslaved, and creating and supporting missionary societies across the nation. The AME Church attracted a somber middle- and upper-class membership and as such was less appealing to the lower and working classes. Yet in both the Baptist and AME churches, both historically and today, people accept Christ as their savior; live for Christ by serving the church, the community, and the world; and share the Gospel with unbelievers. Smaller denominations, including the Church of God in Christ, emphasize charismatic elements of prophesy and healing more so than the African American Baptist and AME churches do.

Consciously or not, African Americans, some even in such mainline churches as the AME Church, have recast the Protestant God of the Trinity as a black deity of African origins who gave humankind the "breath of life." Blending these two religious archetypes of white and black has given African Americans license to embrace a God of contradictions—a God that whites cast as the oppressor and that, at the same time, granted a spiritual or metaphorical, and literal, freedom to blacks. Much like the Hebrews, who spent forty years seeking the Promised Land, the enslaved saw God as a friend, sustainer, redeemer, and liberator. This was true for Aunt Susan Kelly, who was born around 1856 in Guinea, Virginia, who said, "White folks can't pray right to de black man's God. Cain't nobody do it for you. You got to call on God yourself when de spirit tell you to and let God know dat you bin washed free from sin." She worshipped a black God, owning her faith in a personal relationship.[7]

Henry McNeal Turner, the twelfth AME bishop, publicly proclaimed,

> We have as much right biblically and otherwise to believe that God is a Negro, as you buckra, or white, people who have to believe that God is a fine-looking, symmetrical, and ornamented white man. . . . We do not believe that there is any hope for a race of people who do not believe that they look like God. . . . We conclude these remarks by repeating for the information of the Observer what it adjudged us demented for—*God is a Negro*.

The Church of the Living God also decreed that Jesus was black. Black Jews also believed they were the authentic believers and that the historic figure Christ was black. Aunt Susan Kelly and Henry McNeal Turner, among others, described a nuanced black God with whom they had an intimate relationship, a God who was with them in their struggle against racism and segregation. Some African

Americans throughout history have seen themselves in God's own image and have perceived God as someone they could turn to in the struggle against oppression.[8]

As African Americans converted to Christianity, they reinterpreted other icons and rituals of their African ancestors, who treated earth shrines and groves as sacred. Some African Americans have described their religious conversions against the backdrop of nature, in places like blackberry patches and cornfields. *God Struck Me Dead: Voices of Ex-Slaves* (1972), is a remarkable set of conversion narratives collected in the 1930s by African American researchers at Fisk University. Clifton H. Johnson, the editor of the collection, declares that African Americans converted "in the nature of a stroke of lightning which would enter at the top of their head and emerge from their toes. They had to meet God, be baptized by him in the river of Jordan personally, become identified with him."

According to numerous slave narratives, these conversions were initially personal encounters with God, later shared with mothers, fathers, brothers, sisters, neighbors, and even white interviewers employed by the Works Progress Administration, a New Deal government agency that documented oral traditions familiar to Africans and African Americans. The tone, language, and actions of conversions were emotionally and physically expressive, reflecting African spirituality. Nowhere was this more evident than in the shout, a tradition in which African Americans call out, run, roll, and pass out in the Spirit. Though whites also converted in natural settings and have a long history of ecstatic worship, certain recurring actions, images, and symbols made the charismatic experiences of African Americans distinctive in the context of the racial oppression of enslavement.[9]

Nancy Williams, formerly enslaved in Norfolk, Virginia, unceremoniously "got 'ligion," in nature, unfettered by church walls:

Won' no preachers aroun' jes' had get de lawd yo'self. . . Seem like when I lef' de plow de spirit struck me. Den I runned cross de fiel jes' a shoutin'. Jumped over de tall rail fence an' de rails come a-tumblin' on me—all but three. Deed, Ise layin' dere in de weeds dead in sin. I stayed dere; my soul an' body shinin' lak a mawnin star! Soon de white man come a-huntin' for me. See me stretched out dere—an' call name de other niggers, "Git dat darn gal out de weeds! She's daid." . . . When I came to, I jump up off'n dat bench an' start a-runnin' an' shoutin'. Went thew de cawn fiel an' broke down all de cawn. . . . Thought sure Ise in heaven. I had viewed de way in a vision.

Running, tumbling, shining, stretching, dying, jumping, and shouting, Williams experienced the Holy Ghost in a vision. Her old sinful self died in the fields—mirroring the cycles of life and death in the planting season that could have taken place in the fields of Africa or North America—and emerged to a new life and relationship with God, merging African spiritual possession with the indwelling of the Holy Spirit.[10]

Holy Ghost conversions in the fields often shared common elements: working the land; hearing from, acknowledging, and being chosen by God; and accepting the call to ministry. Morte, enslaved in Tennessee, heard a voice while plowing the fields. Thinking it was the master chastising him, Morte jumped. He heard another call and responded, "With this I stopped, dropped the plow, and started running, but the voice kept on speaking to me saying, 'Fear not, my little one, for behold! I come to bring you a message of truth.'" God transformed the fields into a new world or environment. Morte said,

There were plants and animals, and all, even the water where I stooped down to drink, began to cry out, "I am blessed but you are damned! I am blessed but you are damned!" . . . I again prayed, and there came a soft voice saying, "My little one, I have loved you with an everlasting love. You are this day made alive and freed from hell. You are a chosen vessel unto the Lord. . . . Go, and I am with you. Preach the gospel, and I will preach with you. You are henceforth the salt of the earth."[11]

Morte had destroyed much of the corn in his trance. Anticipating a lashing, he told the slaveholder that God had plowed up the corn. The master unexpectedly and tearfully converted after hearing Morte's testimony, giving Morte permission to preach freely rather than plow the fields and allowing him to remain on the land.

Was this fact or fiction? The veracity of this story is less important than its recounting as Morte preached to others, including the slaveholder. The newly converted were mandated in the Bible to teach biblical truths to unbelievers and practice baptism in the name of the Father, Son, and Holy Spirit. Such conversions in natural settings were common among African Americans—both enslaved and free—experiences that they ultimately shared, often orally, with their community.[12]

Carter G. Woodson, a historian and the founder of the Association for the Study of African American Life and History, continued to interpret nature and God during the early twentieth century. His work focused on how Africans' and African Americans' experiences, whether as individuals or as a community, irrevocably connected to the environment in a long history of landlessness. In 1936, Woodson described spirituality, nature, and Africans:

The African in the plains would see that great stretch of land animated with the spirit of the supreme divinity. One living in the forests would find this animation in the trees. The native dwelling near the streams would discern this power in the beneficent developments of this river or a manifestation of evil in the damage which might result in overflow. Rain in one region is a blessing when it makes crops grow and evil in another where floods destroy life and property.[13]

Woodson made groundbreaking contributions to the nascent field of African American studies, although he ironically used the colonized language of animism and nature, Western and racist in scope. His sensibilities had been transformed by whites through enslavement and later in freedom through a system of apartheid that changed the ways he looked at religion and described nature in Africa. By treating African spirituality as one-dimensional he reinforced stereotypes of the primitive and exotic. He also sentimentalized and romanticized the African plains and forests, again a Western perspective.

Molly Jordan, a "mulatto farm woman" at Long Farm in Seaboard, North Carolina, gives a more hands-on account. She was torn in 1938, toward the end of the Great Depression, between her accountability to the government and to the will of God, responsible for the cotton in the fields:

> The Lord made cotton, big stalk and pretty white bolls, and the government says plow it up. It was a sin to let them white locks o' cotton there in the dirt, bad as we needed it. The devil was in it, doggone if it wa'n't! The Bible says the earth is cursed and bear more fruit, and it's come to pass, blest if it hain't. Way I see it, the gov-mint's got us in slavery; they don't whup our backs, but they whup our minds.[14]

Jordan lived in a community of African American farmers who were influenced by religious beliefs and from whom she probably drew at least part of her farming expertise. Conservationists, both

African American and white, understood that continual planting and harvesting of cotton depleted and ruined the soil. But Jordan lived in a white world where she was forced to comply with the government's demand to do the unthinkable—plow up the cotton to increase prices—despite her ethical struggle over stewardship of God-given natural resources.

Toni Morrison, in her 1987 novel *Beloved*, echoes the cultural duality experienced by Jordan. The environment is central to *Beloved*'s plot, with many spiritual references to the woods, water, and animals. Morrison depicts a fictionalized African American church in which the congregation retains Africanisms such as the ring dance among the trees while practicing Protestantism, or "having church." Baby Suggs, "an unchurched preacher," gathered with her church members in a grove, "a wide-open place cut deep in the woods nobody knew for what at the end of a path known only to deer and whoever cleared the land in the first place." She

> told them that the only grace they could have was the grace they could imagine. That if they could not see it, they would not have it. 'Here,' she said, 'in this here place, we flesh; flesh that weeps, laughs; flesh that dances on bare feet in grass. Love it. Love it hard. Yonder they do not love your flesh. They despise it.'[15]

Although social, political, and historical evidence points to whites despising enslaved people's bodies, with the subtext being that whites used those same bodies for sex, reproduction, and labor, Baby Suggs encouraged her congregants to become spiritually whole through self-love, grasping for a self-esteem stolen long ago during enslavement. Morrison refers to God's grace and favor at church among the trees and on the grass. She also flips scripture, rejecting a faith- and theology-based belief in the unseen, instead demanding a tangible reward for African Americans who had endured the horror and indignity of enslavement.

Enslaved people also continued the African practice of meeting in secret wooded places. Such an environmental-spiritual fusion under the trees was flexible as it changed from its spiritual roots in Africa and took on a different meaning from the blended African and Protestant influences in a new freedom. The same was true of so many other African Americans whose spirituality was influenced—really, defined—by African spirituality and Christianity.

The rich legacy of African American spirituality in nature should be reclaimed today. African Americans continue the tradition of membership and service in churches, including predominantly African American churches. Churches can take worship outdoors onto the lawns and in the midst of trees on church property. In urban settings with little greenery, church can happen in nearby parks or trips to wilderness places. After church, those in attendance can continue to fellowship with God while walking the paths and trails of city and state parks. God waits inside the church. S/He is also waiting by a waterfall or under a tree for communion and fellowship with those of us here on earth.

4

Resistance

REBELLION, SUSTENANCE, AND ESCAPE
IN THE WILDERNESS

Joseph dreams that he is a revered priest in West Africa, where his people, the Gruma of the Akan, all call him Minkah, which means "justice." Some of his priestly duties revolve around nature—blessing a field, pouring libations with water onto the ground to revere the ancestors, and tending to the village's earth shrine. Minkah strides through the forests and sees a vision of a tree that weeps and shakes like a small child.

Awaking from his reverie, Joseph realizes that he is this child, who has ended up enslaved. Now, north of the city of Mobile between the Tombigbee and Alabama rivers, he is far from his ancestral home in Africa. Yet he is comforted by the familiarity of leaves falling from the branches of the trees onto the uneven floor, a patchwork of sunlight and shadows in the forest.

Joseph's visions and dreams have momentarily liberated him from the bondage of enslavement with thoughts well

suited for the making of a runaway. Intuitively, he is comfort-
able and familiar with the woods and waterways surrounding the plantation. Joseph runs away for one- to three-day
stretches, relying on his knowledge of nature, which originated in Africa, to survive. The first few times Joseph runs,
Matthew Samford—the slaveholder of a two-hundred-acre
plantation kept productive by seventy-five enslaved people—
tracks him with dogs.

That night under a three-quarter moon, the rags of his
clothes flapping and his bare calloused feet hitting the
ground hard, the woods are filled with the sounds of four
snapping bloodhounds. The adrenaline cocktail of fear and
the rush of air in his lungs slow down when he stumbles
on a fallen rotted log. Jumping to his feet, Joseph listens as
the dogs draw closer. Suddenly, a reeling, ferocious blur, a
mass of teeth, jaws, and muscle, is on him. Joseph cannot
differentiate one beast from another as the hounds bite into
him. Scrambling up a tree, he waits, blood dripping from
the bites covering him from his head to his feet. The whites
arrive at the foot of the tree, Joseph's short-lived sanctuary,
beckoning him to climb down. Joseph jumps down and is
severely beaten. Though he is badly hurt from the violence,
he runs again and again, replaying this bloody tableau in the
woods. After the fifth try, Samford wearies of the chase and
realizes that Joseph returns voluntarily in a day or two anyway, to his woman and children who know to wait because
Joseph always comes back.

Joseph does consider the ultimate escape, flight or an
insurrection, at cross-purposes to his commitment to his
family. News comes from as far away as Toronto of runaways
who make it to freedom but are shocked by the difference in
temperature after leaving the warmth of places like Louisiana

and traveling to the freezing weather of upstate New York and Canada. He also hears of plots planned in cloaked places in the forests throughout the South. Is it true that one prophet had a vision of spirits, blood, and the sun—taken together, the catalyst for the murder of white men, women, and children? Joseph understands the power of the priesthood and prophecy. He understands why a prophet resists oppression. Joseph beckons his people to the arbor to worship, wondering if he should share his plan for revolt in the forest's gloom, just steps away from the fields of the Samford Plantation.

Joseph's experiences were transformed from being primarily spiritual in Africa to having spirituality inform his plans for escape, or resistance, against the backdrop of nature in the South. Much like Joseph, people of African descent in America left the settled places or the civilization of the cabins and fields and entered the wilderness of the forests and swamps for brief periods of respite, to contemplate and plan rebellion, and for more permanent escape from the South to the North.

The biblical Promised Land, otherwise known as Canaan, or Israel, was a settled place for the Hebrews. This land became symbolic among African Americans as a source of hope for a people condemned to enslavement. Much like the Hebrews escaping Egyptian oppressors and wandering the wilderness for forty years to get to Canaan, African Americans left Africa and had to pass through the wilderness—literally, through flight, and metaphorically, when resisting and subverting oppression by whites.

Wilderness evoked both fear and comfort for African Americans. The woods, forests, and swamps were natural places where blacks were hunted and mauled or lynched and hung from trees. Even when these terrible experiences were over, horror and sometimes ambivalence remained. But the wilderness was also a refuge, a place to live long-term, or a place of transition for runaways between the plantation and freedom. Varying responses of anger, ambivalence, comfort, and even appropriation can be traced through the experiences of blacks in Africa and through the Middle Passage, farming, hunting, escapes, and rebellions. Resistance to rural dangers continued during the Jim Crow era, with the Ku Klux Klan assembling in the Southern wilderness. Mixed responses to animals persisted in the face of attack dogs used against Civil Rights demonstrators.

African Americans wrote protest literature, resistance through words, using the settlement and wilderness motifs. David Walker, a Boston businessman best known for the incendiary and provocative pamphlet *Appeal* (1829), and Frederick Douglass used metaphors drawn from the Bible concerning the captivity of the Israelites that reverberated for enslaved African Americans. Walker described Israelites escaping from Egypt, with the sea and land as prominent "characters": "I will not here speak of the destructions which the Lord brought upon Egypt, in consequence of the oppression and consequent groans of the oppressed—of the hundreds and thousands of Egyptians whom God hurled into the Red Sea for afflicting his people and the land."[1]

Douglass expanded on this narrative of exodus and alienation among the Israelites in his speech titled "What to the Slave is the 4th of July?" given on July 4, 1852, in Rochester, New York. Douglass protested the inferior status of African Americans:

> By the rivers of Babylon, there we sat down. Yea! We wept when we remembered Zion. We hanged our harps upon the willows in the midst thereof. For there, they that carried us away captive, required of us a song; and they who wasted us required of us mirth, saying, Sing us one of the songs of Zion.

How can we sing the Lord's song in a strange land? If I forget
thee, O Jerusalem, let my right hand forget her cunning. If I
do not remember thee, let my tongue cleave to the roof of my
mouth.[2]

Ancient Babylon, a strange land to the Hebrews, was a place of
captivity, a place where being Hebrew meant inferior status. This
resonated with African Americans who were enslaved. Zion, or
Israel, including the holy capital of Jerusalem, represented something different: the final stop, the escape from the wilderness and
from persecution by the Babylonians.

Much like protest literature, other written and oral texts, including slave narratives, were tools used by abolitionists in the struggle
against the enslavement of African Americans. Resistance in Africa
and during the Middle Passage was a recurring theme in these
narratives. During the early nineteenth century, Boyrereau Brinch
from Niger was captured by whites and later forced to travel across
the Atlantic to the Caribbean and then North America. In Africa,
Brinch and his companions saw "six or seven animals fastening a
boat, and immediately made towards us." These animals, aliens to
the young men, were whites. Brinch and his friends tried to escape
these unfamiliar creatures who were in pursuit but later encountered "thirty or forty more of the same pale race of white *Vultures*."[3]
The threat posed by whites was synonymous with the malevolence
of the birds.

When the ship arrived in Barbados the comparison to animals
continued in how the Africans were treated by the whites. A slave
named Syneyo went on a work strike to protest the harsh treatment
by the white captors. According to Brinch, Syneyo

rose up, and in his native language, made the following speech
to the captain, which was repeated to him by the interpreter:

"Sir, we will sooner suffer death than submit to such abomina-
ble degradation. The brow of our great father, the sun, frowns
with indignation on beholding the majesty of human nature
abused, as we are, and rendered more brutal than the raven-
ous wild beasts, as ye are. Feel like mortal man, and what I say
may prevent your spirit from being blotted out forever."

Although the whites behaved like "wild beasts," Syneyo tried
using reasoning and threats. Drawing on his African spirituality,
he invoked the wrath of a sun god who would obliterate the whites
from existence. The captain responded with a "countenance that
would terrify a crocodile and a voice like the braying of a Jack-ass."
Syneyo's work strike became a restricted diet forced on him by the
captain, who said,

I will teach you discipline, obedience, and submission, and
what is more, I will learn you your duty. You seem to speak
as though you thought yourself equal to white people, you
Ethiopean [sic] black brute, you shall have but twelve kernels
of corn per day—your breakfast shall be fifty stripes—and if
your work is not done, I leave you to the care of this my overseer, who will deal with you as you deserve.[4]

Rebellions and resistance aboard ships like the *Amistad* were the
substance and inspiration for protest literature by Douglass and slave
narratives by Brinch. In June 1839, José Ruiz and Pedro Montes,
Spanish businessmen, arrived in Havana, Cuba. They purchased
fifty-three blacks, including children, and took them to the *Amistad*,
headed for Puerto Principe in central Cuba. Howard Jones in *Mutiny
on the Amistad: The Saga of a Slave Revolt and Its Impact on American Abolition, Law, and Diplomacy* intimates that rations and weather
helped to trigger the revolt by the Africans: "Thus each black was

allotted only one banana, two potatoes, and a small cup of water per day. Tempers shortened in the tropical heat." One African attempted to take more water and was whipped for it. Cinque, who ultimately became the leader of the revolt, became concerned about the whites' objectives when one shipmate pantomimed that the Africans would end up as salted meat to be eaten by cannibalistic whites. Jones adds, "A storm soon hit, blackening the night and forcing the crew to lower the sails for hours until it passed over. Around 4:00 a.m., with the sky still rainy and darkened by heavy clouds, Ruiz and Montes were suddenly awakened by screams of 'Murder!'" Cinque and the band of Africans murdered all but two whites and took the *Amistad*.

None of the Africans had experience with navigation or seafaring, so what seemed to them a watery wilderness lay ahead. Cinque forced one of the whites to "sail the *Amistad* into the sun" with the hope of returning back to Mother Africa. Along with dehydration and starvation, they faced another storm, which allowed the whites to lower the sails and slow any progress to Africa. Because the Africans did not know better, the ship ended up off the shores of Long Island in August. They were captured, jailed, and tried in New York. Ultimately, Cinque and the others were freed.[5]

Living out his own civilization and wilderness narrative, Cinque returned to Africa after the trial, going to Sierra Leone with missionaries, unlike most Africans who landed in the Americas and the Caribbean. Transplanted and enslaved, Africans lived out the metaphors of settled places and the desert wilderness in which the Hebrews wandered. People of African descent worked as domestics in houses or as agricultural laborers on slaveholders' land. Blacks worked either as specialists or in gangs on the land. Particular expertise, including constructing and repairing irrigation systems, was required in many aspects of rice production. Specialized knowledge was less important for African Americans working in teams planting and picking cotton.

Against this backdrop, African Americans practiced guerrilla tactics—an environmental terrorism of sorts—taking back some of the power drained from them by enslavement. In the fields, forms of resistance included slowdowns and work stoppages. Some took their time picking cotton and cropping tobacco. Others feigned illness to shorten a workday. The enslaved broke and lost tools. Livestock and working animals were abused, another way to rebel against slaveholders. African Americans did not care about rationing the feed for the animals, let livestock run wild, and ignored the safety of the work animals. And why shouldn't they when Africans Americans were treated like chattel?[6]

Beyond the fields, hunting proved to be a form of resistance. Enslaved people shared their game with one another to support and strengthen the group. They skirted around the white-dominated hunting system and went after game that the slaveholders would not miss or desire—pests like foxes, raccoons, opossum, and squirrels. Much of the hunting was done at night or on Sundays when the enslaved were free from picking cotton and chopping sugarcane. A few of them had access to guns, though most used traps and snares. They hunted secretly and used the time in the woods and swamps for leisure, away from the plantations and farms. In this way, the enslaved made the slaveholders' spaces their own through community, secrecy, and recreation.[7]

Running away took resistance to another level. Maroons, fugitives who were once enslaved and organized independent communities in the Caribbean and the United States, remained hidden from whites. Individuals such as Harriet Tubman and Frederick Douglass also ran off to urban places in the South, the Northeast, and Canada. The first Maroons in Jamaica, West Indies, escaped enslavement as they used the landscape to evade the British and conceal themselves in the interior of the island in the Blue Mountains. Their experiences reflect those of runaways in the American South. Kenneth M. Bilby describes the Maroons' surroundings in *True-Born Maroons*:

> The rebels had every topographical advantage, for they held possession of the "Cockpits." Those highlands are furrowed through and through, as by an earthquake, with a series of gaps and ravines, resembling the California cañons, or those similar fissures in various parts of the Atlantic States, known to local fame either poetically as ice-glens, or symbolically as purgatories. These Jamaica chasms vary from two hundred yards to a mile in length; the rocky walls are fifty or a hundred feet high, and often absolutely inaccessible, while the passes at each end admit but one man at a time. They are thickly wooded, wherever trees can grow; water flows within them; and they often communicate with one another, forming a series of traps for an invading force.[8]

The Jamaican Maroons were described as "wild Children of the Mist," apropos since the rebels used their surroundings like phantoms to resist colonial control. Their metaphorical flight from Egypt through the wilderness was marked by place-names such as Old Abraham and Stone Wall, before they reached the Promised Land, where Maroon society developed, in Nanny Town.

After the Maroons escaped, they had to survive off the land. They scavenged for food such as cacoon beans from the vine and hearts of palm, and they hunted wild hogs using dogs to track them in the forest, then shooting their prey and butchering it with machetes. Herbs from plants also served their medicinal needs, as they were so far away from the influences of Western medicine. The Maroons' ability to live off the land, often by eating raw food, gave them an advantage over the British soldiers in pursuit, who relied on rations and hot food. Maroons also used the rivers to escape the British and to fish for food. Finally, the forest served as camouflage from the seeking eyes of the British troops. Nancy Prince, an African American missionary, said, "These Maroons would secrete themselves in trees, and arrest the whites as they passed along."[9]

Shifting from the Caribbean back to North America, men like Gabriel Prosser, Denmark Vesey, and Nat Turner instigated rebellions. Turner, who planned and led an insurrection in Southampton, Virginia, in 1831, blended the redemptive narrative of Jesus Christ's ministry in the New Testament with the civilization/wilderness template of the Old Testament. Turner was strongly influenced by Christianity, saying,

> My grandmother, who was very religious, and to whom I was much attached,—my master, who belonged to the church, and other religious persons who visited the house, and whom I often saw at prayers, noticing the singularity of my manners, I suppose, and my uncommon intelligence for a child, remarked I had too much sense to be raised, and if I was, I would never be of any service to any one as a slave.

He claimed to hear from God and accepted the call of the prophet, waiting and praying for a few years. His cue to launch a rebellion came in the form of prophetic visions:

> I saw white spirits and black spirits engaged in battle, and the sun was darkened—the thunder rolled in the Heavens, and the blood flowed in streams . . . And I looked and saw the forms of men in different attitudes—and there were lights in the sky to which the children of darkness gave other names than what they really were—for the lights of the Savior's

hands, stretched forth from east to west, even as they were extended on the cross on Calvary for the redemption of sinners . . . While laboring in the field, I discovered drops of blood on the corn as though it were dews from heaven . . . I then found on the leaves in the woods hieroglyphic characters, and numbers, with the forms of men in different attitudes, portrayed in blood, and representing the figures I had seen before in the heavens.

Turner led approximately forty insurrectionists toward the town of Jerusalem, Virginia. The coincidence of the name of the nearest town once again evokes the civilization/wilderness template of the Promised Land. The band was scattered by militia, but Turner managed to escape. He cloaked himself in nature, hiding under a downed tree.[10]

Harriet Tubman, born in the early nineteenth century and enslaved in Maryland, took resistance beyond the borders of the Southern farms, plantations, and towns. Following the North Star, she crossed difficult and unknown landscapes on her own to Delaware and Pennsylvania. When dark clouds obscured Tubman's guiding star, abolitionists pointed her in the right direction along the Underground Railroad, or she felt for moss on tree trunks, knowing that the plant grows on the north side of trees. She landed in Philadelphia, Pennsylvania, a place that stood in stark contrast to her rural beginnings. Later, Tubman earned the moniker Moses of her people by returning to Maryland to lead others to the Promised Land in the North. But first the fugitives had to pass through the wilderness with a gun-toting Tubman. Ultimately, she settled down even farther north, in Canada, having decided, according to historian Catherine Clinton, that "Canada was the new Canaan, and Niagara her new River Jordan."[11] The Israelites crossed the Jordan

River to get to Canaan (modern-day Israel), passing from wilderness to civilization.

Harriet Tubman and other runaways were often pursued by slaveholders and their dogs. The significance of dogs can be traced throughout narratives of enslavement, and even today dogs typify for many African Americans the ambiguity of nature defined by ethnicity, race, and racism. Looking to ancient Rome, seventeenth-century England, and the nineteenth-century United States, we see that dogfights were deemed acceptable. More specifically for African Americans, bloodhounds meant capture for many runaways; for others, the animals loyally tracked prey and herded livestock.[12]

So it is no coincidence that history and culture continue to influence the treatment of domesticated animals even today by people around the world, including African Americans in the South. In 2007, football star Michael Vick was the focus of the media when it was discovered that dogfights were taking place on his property. He was ultimately convicted of cruelty to animals in Virginia, adding another layer, violence against animals, to the environmental history of domesticated animals. In an unfortunate historical turnabout, dogs were once used to brutalize runaways and civil rights advocates; years later, Vick and his guests were brutalizing, even killing, dogs.

Though such behavior is inexcusable, a long history and complex relationship between African Americans and their animals bear more analysis, which the media missed in their repetitive coverage. Vick was publicly vilified as a prosperous black man who repeated what was probably a learned behavior that was typical, albeit illegal today, of African American and white men who bonded together by participating in a dogfighting ritual that goes back through the millennia.

A living example of the civilization and wilderness metaphors, Vick began on the edges of society as an African American man before his professional football career propelled him into the spotlight and into a Promised Land. For a time, Vick returned to the edges in prison, shamed by his brutal acts against dogs. Looking to the fictional character Joseph, who was stripped of his manhood when dogs tore at him and whites beat him, has social history repeated or turned back on itself?

5

Preservation

BLENDING THE PRACTICAL AND THE PURIST

It is 1917. Surrounded by yellow pine in Alabama, Lola Lampre sits in the woods with the prickly needles beneath her bare brown legs. She is far away from her distant ancestor Minkah but has only just left the house of her father, Owen Samford. Lola was the last child born to her mother, who died during childbirth. She and her seven siblings helped their father in the fields or the house as they sharecropped land owned by the white side of the Samford family.

Lola thought she was escaping a hard life working with her brothers and sisters when she married Edgar Lampre. Not so. She now lives in a small tented community with her husband, who works in the mill. Lola goes into the nearby sawmill town to clean houses for three white women, thankfully returning home at night and escaping the groping hands of her employers' husbands.

It is Sunday, her day off, so Lola just sits. There is no wind, so the woods are strangely silent. She looks up and sees the sky and clouds between branches of the ancient evergreens. The mill is not churning, not cutting wood on what is a holy day for many in the South. So Lola has this brief respite; her husband is off fishing so they have something to eat tonight. But she knows that inevitably the saws and axes will destroy her little patch of sacred wooded sanctuary. Her husband does not share her love for nature because the trees represent hard work in the summer heat and humidity in the Alabama woods and mill. And this life is not permanent but transitory. They will live there only as long as the trees remain for the cutting.

M uch as Lola's moments combined reverie and reality, practical preservation drew on conservation and nature study—a formal curricula from grade school through higher education that emphasized appreciation of nature—to form a distinct tradition of preservation-conservation. The brand of practical preservation practiced in rural living in the South was part of the broader preservationist ideology and movement, the latter national and mainstream in scope. The 1916 publication *Negro Farmer and Messenger* highlighted how African Americans were encouraged to blend environmental whimsy with practicality:

> Successful living in any place depends upon the spiritual and mental attitude. One must be in sympathy with the natural environment in which he finds himself . . . . They must be open minded and try to learn whatever they can that will improve farm conditions . . . When they are convinced of these things and have learned to love the wind and the rain, the growing things, the birds, and all the rest, the dawn, the early morning

ordor [sic], and to find each part of the day, each twilight, and
each nightfall filled with wonders, they will know how to live
on a farm and how to make a living on a farm will be less of
a problem.[1]

Preservationists, often white, were purists who embraced an aesthetic ideal of nature. They promoted restricted access to nature and
protection of endangered flora and fauna in order to maintain or
re-create pristine environments. Preservationists fervently argued
that people should not disturb natural areas, including forests and
waterways. However, although white preservationists, often elite and
privileged, embraced this ideal of nature, they also protected, studied, and played in the midst of endangered and not-so-endangered
flora and fauna. John Muir, a pioneer of the preservationist movement and founder of the Sierra Club, lobbied to protect what he saw
as pristine natural settings by creating national park status for California's Yosemite and Hetch Hetchy valleys. In a letter to Mrs. Ezra S.
Carr, a confidante, Muir said, "I'm beneath that grand old pine that
I have heard so often at night and in the day. It sings grandly now,
every needle sun-thrilled and shining and responding tunefully to
the azure sky."

Wealthy white women in the Audubon Society were also active in
the preservationist movement. As members of the middle and upper
classes, they had the personal and economic autonomy necessary to
participate in women's organizations such as the national General
Federation of Women's Clubs, which guarded exotic plumed birds,
coveted for the feathers so popular for decorating hats during that
period.[2]

White preservationist ideology along with African influences certainly shaped the African American experience. The Khoesaan of
Zimbabwe, a hunter-gatherer society, practiced something akin to
nature appreciation. They painted the interior walls of the Matapos

caves in Zimbabwe; the best examples are found in the Nswatugi cave. One such painting is of a giraffe and zebra in motion. Without the benefit of a written record, some observers argue that the Khoesaan expressed an appreciation for the beauty of the animals, while others argue that the Khoesaan wished to control nature by attempting to leave permanent marks on the rock walls. I support a variation of these two arguments; since the Khoesaan did not consider the giraffe and zebra to be sources of meat or even skins, critical to their hunter-gatherer subsistence, control became moot. Without the hunt, the Khoesaan responded with an aesthetic appreciation, depicting the giraffe and zebra through art.

Africans incorporated nature's forces and materials into their belief systems, which differed from place to place and ethnic group to ethnic group. Enslaved people certainly had a connection with nature, and some of them were African born. For example, Old Uncle Louis was enslaved in Alabama during the nineteenth century and was described as a "Guinea nigger," likely a reflection of his African ancestry. Louis boasted of his hunting skills. He was also known for his "great knowledge of wild plants" and "claimed to understand the language of birds and beasts."[3]

Louis blended conservation with wilderness appreciation, a study in contradictions, though seamless in his recounting, that would continue later in similar ways among a generation of African Americans. Louis described his enchantment with nature as follows:

> [D]e woods seems to call me. When de fall insec's is singin' in de grass an' the 'simmons is getting soft an' de leaves is beginning to turn, I jes natcherly has ter go. De wild sloes, de red haws an' de crab apples is ripe. De walnuts an de hickory nuts an de beach mast drappin' an de blue smoke comes over de woods, an de woods birds an de yard birds goes souf wid de

cranes an ducks an wil' geese and de blackbirds an de crows
goes in droves—it seems lack all dat is jes callin' me.

Louis lived in a "big green oak tree" where no one could see him,
and he constructed a bed from poles and grass. When he strayed
from the tree, he stretched out to fish and "listen to de birds and
critters talkin'." The old man also said, "a chickadee tole me you [a
Works Progress Administration interviewer] was comin' long befo'
I seen you. Den a jay bird caught a sight of you an he tole me." It
is fitting and contradictory that this nature lover both hunted and
befriended the inscrutable owl and the imposing hawk.

Uncle Louis's memories of enslavement were as insightful as
preservationist depictions of nature by African American novelists
in the early twentieth century, including W. E. B. DuBois's *The Quest
of the Silver Fleece*, Zora Neale Hurston's *Their Eyes Were Watching God*
(1937), and Jean Toomer's *Cane* (1923).

For example, in *Cane*, Toomer's elegant poetry and prose chroni-
cle the life of African Americans in piney Georgia. Highlights of his
own life defined his fiction. He was born on December 26, 1894,
in New Orleans to Nina Pinchback, the daughter of Pinckney B. S.
Pinchback, an African American who became acting governor of
Louisiana during the Reconstruction era, and Nathan Toomer, who
ultimately abandoned his family and was the son of a Georgia plantation owner. As the grandson of B. S. Pinchback, Toomer spent part
of his young life among an elite caste of educated and well-heeled
African Americans—a status that initially distanced them from
working-class African Americans—common throughout the South
but very pronounced among Louisiana's black Creoles. At age four-
teen Toomer left his mother and stepfather in New York and went to
live with his uncle Bismark in a socioeconomically mixed neighborhood in Washington, D.C. Later, after abandoning agricultural work

at the University of Wisconsin and Massachusetts College of Agriculture, along with the bodybuilding program at American College of Physical Training in Chicago, the biology program at the University of Chicago, the sociology program at New York University, and psychology classes at the City College of New York, Toomer began to formulate his craft by reading and writing. These early experiences led to a stint in 1921 as an interim principal of an agricultural and industrial school in Sparta, Georgia, the setting for *Cane*.[4]

While there, Toomer worked together many fictionalized layers into what became the tales of African Americans in the Georgia forests, where capitalists and the government cut down lumber. His vision of the forest was both sacrosanct and pragmatic, detailed in both the beauty of the pine and the rape of the forest for profit. Around him, men mangled and stripped the forest, plunging axes into living tree trunks while sawmills spewed and burned after sawing wood, the middle stage of the lumbering process.

Although Toomer does not specifically mention the harvesting of turpentine in *Cane*, the industry expanded into Georgia during the period in which he wrote the short stories and poetry. Turpentine workers chipped at trees and used metal cups to collect the turpentine and rosin. The industry left scarred trees that were vulnerable to wood-boring insects such as the ips beetle, turpentine borer, and black turpentine beetle.[5]

Toomer's work describes a sawmill rising from the Georgia landscape. Much of North Carolina's forests had already been stripped by the late nineteenth century, with little thought of seeding replacement crops. The lumber industry then moved on to Florida and Georgia—the latter was Toomer's home for a short period—continuing large-scale deforestation throughout the early twentieth century. Sawmills across the South spewed dark smoke from stacks. Although visually arresting, the mills polluted the air, typical of much industry during the twentieth century. During the many stages of taking the lumber, living trees were chopped or sawed; the logs were floated on rivers or transported by rail; the timber was cut into boards upon arrival at the sawmills unless the pine stood close by; and the cut boards were transported by rail and sold to customers who built homes, schoolhouses, town halls, and other buildings.[6]

Toomer's backwoods tales are set against the Georgia pines, an enthralling and damaged place depicted in "Karintha," a short story, and "Georgia Dusk," a poem. Karintha, a once virginal girl taken by or offering herself up to men, is a metaphor for purity and pollution in nature. At twelve, a child prematurely hastened into womanhood, she plays within eyeshot of smoke seeping from a sawmill, a hint of things to come: "At sunset, when there was no wind, and the pine-smoke from over by the sawmill hugged the earth and you couldnt [sic] see more than a few feet in front, her sudden darting past you was a bit of vivid color, like a black bird that flashes in light."

The black bird, a metaphor for Karintha's fate, represents evil or bad luck. Toomer continues:

> Karintha is a woman. She who carries beauty, perfect as dusk when the sun goes down. . . . A child fell out of her womb onto a bed of pine-needles in the forest. Pine-needles are smooth and sweet. They are elastic to the feet of rabbits. . . . A sawmill was nearby. Its pyramidal sawdust pile smouldered [sic]. It is a year before one completely burns out. Meanwhile, the smoke curls up and hangs in old wraiths about the trees, curls up, and spreads itself out over the valley.

Many paramours want Karintha even in childhood, with the outcome being a baby, a ubiquitous dilemma for girl-women. Toomer's tale of light and dark, good and evil, leaves the reader with one question: Was the birth, set amid pretty pine and scampering rabbits, a scene that quickly shifted to dark smoke wafting from a sawmill, a blessing or a curse?[7]

Toomer frames "Georgia Dusk" in this preservationist-conservationist ambiguity, as he conjures up a sublime moment of men leaving a sawmill at the end of a mundane workday: "Their voices rise . . . the pine trees are guitars / Strumming, pine-needles fall like sheets of rain . . . Their voices rise . . . the chorus of the cane / Is caroling a vesper to the stars." Destined to return to another monotonous shift the next day, Toomer's sawmill workers are temporarily divested of their cares as they leave a place that is oppressive to the men and destructive to the trees. Their song of expectancy intermingles with the celestial melody created by the sway of the pine and the cane.[8]

Artist John Thomas Biggers painted a more expansive interpretation of blacks and the environment than Toomer's local Georgian landscape. Biggers integrates references to Africa and even the origins of life into the African American experience in his mural *Web of Life* (1958). The mural reflects experiences from Biggers's youth during the first part of the twentieth century, drawing on the transformative influences of his father, his mentor Viktor Lowenfeld, and Africa. The artist was born in rural Gastonia, North Carolina, on April 13, 1924. His father wore many hats, but those of Baptist preacher and farmer were probably most influential to the spirituality of his son's painting. Biggers attended Hampton Institute, a historically black university in Virginia, to learn a trade but switched to art when he attended a class taught by Lowenfeld, a Jewish refugee from Austria. Through Lowenfeld's tutelage and mentoring, Biggers began to explore African art, an influence that deepened when Biggers traveled to West Africa as a United Nations Educational, Scientific, and Cultural Organization (UNESCO) fellow in 1957.

The Web of Life, one of Biggers's most prominent murals, draws upon his years in the rural South. In one section, African American farmers cast seeds upon a field recently cultivated by a horse and plow. Biggers parallels the labor of farmers in America with women carrying baskets on their heads filled with the harvest and walking past another field in another place and perhaps another time in Africa. He depicts the origins of life, another link to both Africans and African Americans, in two ways. To the left are icebergs, with the sea teeming with fish just below. To the right are fish, an octopus, and a starfish being nourished by a waterfall, water being universally and metaphorically the source of life. In the center of the mural, a mother suckles her baby, also symbolic of birth and life. A naked man and woman, whose union is the source of human life, stretch above Mother Earth and her child. Taken in its entirety, Biggers's rendering knits together the spiritual connections in nature based on his father's teachings and African influences instilled by Lowenfeld and his trip to Africa.[9]

African Americans drew from the mainstream in the form of the purist preservation preached by white environmentalists such as John Muir. But as people of African descent they also drew on African traditions and aesthetics, resulting in the practice of a preservation-conservation distinctive to their experiences, set primarily here in the American South.

6

Conservation

AN AFRICAN LEGACY OF WORKING THE LAND

With a sloped back, cracked hands, and veined and muscled arms, Destin Samford, a sharecropper now generations away from Minkah, his African ancestor, cultivates a field in Alabama. In August, he turns away from the white-orange sun fading against a wine-colored sky to scan the earth speckled with cotton bolls framed by green leaves. He bends, back curved and crooked in places, to pull a boll of cotton from the tough spiny casing, marking the beginning of the harvest. Come January, he raises a cupped calloused hand filled with soil and gauges its tilth against the fading sunlight. Speaking softly into the breeze, he wonders if the weariness creeping from his hands to his arms, shoulders, back, legs, and feet will prevent him from finishing the last task of the day: collecting stubble and leaves to mix with barnyard manure for fertilizer. Months later, in May, with harvesting but a memory, he leans his muscled arms into the plow's wooden handles, smoothed by time and his exertions, to prepare the land for yet another season of cotton cultivation as the failing light turns to darkness.

This archetypal sharecropper reflects efforts in conservation and agricultural techniques, a blended rural preservation-conservation practiced by some African American farmers during many a planting season in the South. Enslaved people and sharecroppers, who used their backs, hands, and arms as their most important tools, passed their farming practices and knowledge from one generation to the next. African Americans terraced hills, planted hot and cold beds, operated cultivators and plows, pushed forks, and pulled rakes. They used these techniques to practice conservation and agricultural methods despite the complications of race and racism.[1]

Much of this knowledge began in Africa, where some Africans practiced environmentally friendly conservation that was synonymous with subsistence farming. Such practices were continued in America by the enslaved and ultimately exploited by slaveholders. Enslaved people appropriated their own patches of land around cabins and on the edges of slaveholders' fields. Later, sharecroppers toiled alongside their wives and children to maintain productivity, profitability, and their own social hierarchy. Confronted with the barriers of an economic and social system dominated by whites, African American farmers used their hands and cultivators as tools to harness and redefine nature, to apply conservation and agricultural principles—some friendly to the environment and others not.[2]

African Americans, like other Americans and also Africans, practiced soil conservation—the practice of rotating cash crops like cotton and tobacco with cowpeas, for example, which returned precious nitrogen to the soil. Conservation was ostensibly the wise use of natural resources for the benefit of future generations; however, some conservationists, veiled in altruism at the turn of the twentieth century, were often self-serving, exploiting natural resources such as water for irrigation, timber for construction, and coal for heat. Farmers practiced soil conservation that returned fertility to the soil in order to improve the quality and quantity of their crops. Agricultural techniques at the same time differed from and were synonymous with conservation practices whether or not the results were restorative. For example, deep plowing, an agricultural technique, destroyed the soil, while terracing the land and rotating crops conserved the soil, the latter being cornerstones of conservation methods.[3]

African Americans who practiced conservation paralleled the efforts of mainstream American conservationists in the early 1900s. White conservationists promoted the use of the land, timber, water, and grass for future generations. President Theodore Roosevelt was one prominent white crusader of this early conservation. Roosevelt and those in his administration combined a sense of morality with a desire for reform and science as the means to protect water, forests, and minerals.[4]

Looking back and across the Atlantic Ocean, Africans also sought to improve the soil. This broad point does not require a claim of ancestral connection between the peoples of Zimbabwe, for example, and African American farmers but provides evidence to consider concerning the conservation and agricultural techniques that were actually practiced in Africa.

Near what is now Nyanga, a town in northeastern Zimbabwe, Africans cultivated grains, legumes, and tubers on the hills rather than in the lowlands to escape flooding during the late Iron Age circa A.D. 1300. They farmed on terraced hills, carving out narrow ledges, which diminished soil erosion, rather than plant below. This left little space for plowing, and so they used hand tools such as hoes and rakes, which ultimately enhanced soil fertility. Along with terraces, they constructed cultivation ridges by elevating the soil to safeguard against flooding and built hydraulic works comprising a series of water furrows to transport water to their crops. Africans of Nyanga also practiced intercropping, mixing grains and legumes together, which returned nitrogen to the soil, and crop rotation, which replenished the fields.[5]

Amma So of Senegal practiced intercropping maize with *gajaba* or sorghum, a method that was highly regarded but not easily repeated by neighboring farmers between the late eighteenth and the early nineteenth centuries. This period was closer in time to the experiences of African Americans in the American South, and Senegal was an important source in the transatlantic slave trade; thus this connection is perhaps less tenuous than those comparisons with Nyanga. Amma So's experience is described in Adrian Adams and Jaabe So's *A Claim to Land by the River*:

> When the ears of maize were still young, he would ask Seexu Jomo to lend him some *taalibo*, and they would weed the maize-field until it was perfectly clean. Then he would sow *gajaba* under the maize plants. When the maize was ripe and dry, he would harvest it and stack it on high ground, then weed the *gajaba*.[6]

It was, in fact, the *taalibo*, or enslaved people, who cultivated the fields under the direction of Amma So and returned nutrients to soil depleted by years of farming. These techniques were also known to some Senegambians and other peoples in West Africa, all the main source of enslaved laborers who traveled with their agricultural skills to the American South.

Historians argue that African Americans, particularly the enslaved, continued the agricultural practices of African ancestors like Amma So—practices completely alien to the white slaveholders, managers, and overseers. Enslaved people who worked daily in rice fields or with other crops understood the environment better than the slaveholders because the enslaved worked with their own hands as they stood hip-deep in the water that sustained rice production.[7]

Farmers in the rural South, including African Americans, planted a variety of cash crops, such as cotton, tobacco, sugarcane, and indigo. The techniques required to sustain Southern agriculture, both great and small, varied from one type of plant to another. As the primary source of labor during and after enslavement, African Americans toiled for hours in the humid heat and bitter cold from daybreak to sundown, bending, stooping, picking, plucking, and lifting.

Cotton production was one of the most labor-intensive and lucrative crops, outside of sugarcane, which was more of an economic gamble from planting the cane to processing it into sugar. Work in the cotton fields began in winter to prepare for planting in the spring. After the seeds were planted and sprouting, the new plants were thinned and the weeds pulled. When the cotton bolls matured in summer, they had to be picked, a process that pricked fingers. Whether as a family unit, as wage laborers, or even earlier as the enslaved, African Americans all filled their sacks with cotton or chopped cane.[8]

Enslaved people sustained and practiced agricultural methods throughout the South in states like Georgia, South Carolina, and Virginia. In the rice culture of All Saints Parish in South Carolina, slaveholders purchased Africans who were experts in rice planting and cultivation. Enslaved people in Georgia picked caterpillars and grasshoppers from cotton by hand because arsenic was not yet being used as a pesticide; it stands to reason Africans probably did much the same.

In 1861, May Satterfield, who was born enslaved in Lynchburg, Virginia, described an agricultural method that was less scientific and more a community or folk tradition: "All plants bearing crops above ground, such as wheat, corn, etc., must be seeded on the increase, while those underground—potatoes, etc.—on the decrease of the moon." Whether Satterfield ascribed to fanciful folk traditions or legitimate agricultural techniques, slaveholders often deferred to such knowledge.

In addition, Marrinda Jane Singleton, from Norfolk, Virginia, said, "Kin use nearly every finding in de hog, even what you find in de intrels, dey use now dese new days fer fertilizer. Stuff used as manure on yer lands." Did her ancestors mix hog intestines with biodegradable scraps like vegetables, leaves, and grass, a precursor to modern-day composting in the suburban garden? It would seem likely.[9]

Between enslavement and the early twentieth century, African Americans eagerly sought land rights. In the early years of Reconstruction, the Bureau of Refugees, Freedmen, and Abandoned Lands, or the Freedmen's Bureau, which operated from 1865 to 1868, supervised or arbitrated wage and sharecropping contracts between formerly enslaved people and slaveholders. Unfortunately for blacks, Southern whites loosely interpreted the contracts, leaving the Bureau powerless and fleecing the freedmen, who in turn often fled their contracts. The promise of forty acres and a mule outlined in Union general William Tecumseh Sherman's Special Field Orders, No. 15 seemed a short-term and local answer. It enabled African Americans to continue to farm in Georgia and its islands, but it was not a panacea for landlessness among African Americans across the South.[10]

Ultimately, only a few African Americans owned farms and possessed equipment, barns, houses, and mules after Reconstruction. In Georgia, as was true of much of the South, African Americans remained in or returned to farming after emancipation, primarily as tenants and wage laborers with limited alternatives. In 1900,

of approximately 250,000 African American farmers, more than
170,000 were wage laborers, 70,000 were tenants and cash renters,
and fewer than 10,000 were farm owner-operators. Tenants contrac-
tually agreed to share a portion of their profits with the landowners.
According to Carter G. Woodson, there were five classes of tenants,
including

> share tenants who pay a certain share of the crop for the use of
> the land but furnish their work animals; croppers whose work
> animals are furnished by the planters; share-cash tenants who
> pay the rent partly in cash and partly in products; cash tenants
> who pay cash altogether for the use of the land; and standing
> renters who pay a stated amount of farm products for the use
> of the farm land.

Unfortunately, most tenants who became indebted were forced to
submit to one option: purchasing seed, food, and tools from white
landowners' stores before crops were even harvested. Whether
cheated and exploited by whites or legitimately in debt, African
Americans struggled to survive.[11]

W. E. B. DuBois, Clementine Hunter, Ned Cobb, and Richard
Bush Woodford, a writer and contributor to the rural newspaper the
Southern Workman, published by Hampton Institute, told their own
stories of preservation-conservation of the land in prose, art, and
practice during the early twentieth century. In *The Souls of Black Folk*,
W. E. B. DuBois expresses an empathy, melancholy, and nostalgia for
the land, giving it human qualities: "The poor land groans with its
birth-pains, and brings forth scarcely a hundred pounds of cotton
to the acre, where fifty years ago it yielded eight times as much." He
goes on to describe one man's hatred of the land, harvested through
violence and racism during enslavement:

"This land was a little Hell," said a ragged, brown, and grave-faced man to me. We were seated near a roadside blacksmith-shop, and behind was the ruin of some master's home. "I've seen niggers drop dead in the furrow but they were kicked aside, and the plough never stopped. And down in the guard-house, there's where the blood ran."

In *The Quest of the Silver Fleece* DuBois also describes an ethereal place, though in reality cotton cultivation was hardscrabble:

We turn up the earth and sow it soon after Christmas. Then pretty soon there comes a sort of greenness on the black land and it swells and grows and—shivers. Then stalks shoot up with three or four leaves. That's the way it is, now, see? After that we chop out the weak stalks, and the strong ones grow tall and dark, till I think it must be like the ocean—all green and billowy; then come little flecks here and there and the sea is all filled with flowers—flowers like little bells, blue and purple and white.[12]

Though DuBois emphasized conservation by pointing out the diminishing returns brought on by excessive cotton harvests, he also hinted at a philosophy of preservation by describing the environment in human and lyrical ways.[13]

During the twentieth century, Clementine Hunter painted charmed rural scenes of African Americans on the Melrose Planta-tion, which was located along the Cane River in Louisiana. In some ways her paintings are similar to DuBois' words. In *Pickin' Cotton* she creates a self-portrait, a woman in a red hat picking cotton in the fields with geese—commonly used across the South to eat the grass shoots before chemicals were used for that purpose—off to one side.[14]

Other African Americans also used natural methods. In 1914 *The Negro Farmer* staff urged African American farmers to apply organic farming methods rather than chemical pesticides: "Turn chickens and turkeys into the orchards to help destroy insects, but do not let them roost in the trees. The guinea, ducks, and geese are also splendid insect hunters."[15] Birds served as a form of natural insect control in the orchard. According to Clementine Hunter, the same was true in the fields.

The Alabama sharecropper Ned Cobb, practicing a rural preservation-conservation in the hope of producing an abundant cotton harvest, shifted from protecting to later destroying the environment. Cobb first used an organic method of handpicking or plucking boll weevils from cotton, although he grudgingly shifted to the use of arsenic to control the boll weevil after emancipation. He envisioned the boll weevil, his enemy, as a sentient creature: Using an environmentally conscious method of pest control on the "sneakin devil" or boll weevil, Cobb only harvested six bales of cotton, a financial loss in 1923: "Didn't use no poison at that time, just pickin' up squares. All you could do was keep them boll weevils from hatchin' out and goin' back up on that cotton. Couldn't kill 'em." He continued to struggle with this environmental-ethical dilemma: "I was industrious enough to do somethin about the boll weevil without bein' driven to it. Picked up them squares and destroyed 'em, destroyed the weevil eggs. Sometimes, fool around there and see a old weevil himself."[16]

Cobb ultimately decided to destroy the pests by applying arsenic or powdered arsenate with a spray.

When I seed I couldn't defeat the boll weevil by pickin' up squares, I carried poison out to the field and took me a crocus sack, one of these thin crocus sacks, put my poison in there enough to poison maybe four or five rows and just walk, walk,

walk; shake that sack over the cotton and when I'd look back,
heap of times, that dust flyin' every which way and the breeze
blowin', that cotton would be white with dust, behind me. Get
to the end, turn around and get right on the next row. Sometimes I'd just dust every other row and the dust would carry
over the rows I passed.

He also followed the recommendations of government entomolo-
gists to burn the infested cotton plants after the harvest to destroy
any remaining pests.[17]

As late as 1969, Cobb understood the ill effects of drifting arsenic, which tainted the soil and the water supply and, worse, poi-
soned people: "And I'd wear a mouth piece over my mouth—still
that poison would get in my lungs and bother me. Now they got
tractors fixed with boxes to elevate that poison out, carry poison
four rows, six rows at one run." At a minimum, he and his family
were exposed to arsenic inhalation and skin damage. Skin lesions,
anemia, renal damage, and lung cancer were symptomatic of lower
doses of the poison. Higher and more lethal exposure meant rapid
death. Ultimately, his family's economic need outweighed his health
and environmental concerns. Hunter and Cobb exemplified the
tug of preservation-conservation in rural farming with empathy
toward the environment standing at odds with practical agricultural
practices.[18]

Richard Bush Woodford focused specifically on conservation. In
an article titled "Rotation of Crops and its Relation to Soil Fertility"
in a 1903 issue of *Southern Workman*, Woodford says, "When we
speak of rotation or change of crops, we mean the planting of crops
so that the same cultivated crop does not appear twice in succession."
He offers several reasons for farmers to implement this agricultural

method: some plants, particularly legumes, are better than others at extracting nutrients from the soil; monoculture attracts insects and fungus; and many weeds are destroyed with crop rotation.[19]

In his 2003 novel *The Known World*, Edward P. Jones depicts the life of an enslaved man with an intimate knowledge of the earth, a reflection of preservation-conservation practiced by African Americans.

> Moses closed his eyes and bent down and took a pinch of the soil and ate it with no more thought than if it were a spot of cornbread. He worked the dirt around in his mouth and swallowed, leaning his head back and opening his eyes in time to see the strip of sun fade to dark blue and then to nothing. . . . This was July, and July dirt tasted even more like sweetened metal than the dirt of June or May. Something in the growing crops unleashed a metallic life that only began to dissipate in mid-August, and by harvest time that life would be gone altogether, replaced by a sour moldiness he associated with the coming of fall and winter, the end of a relationship he had begun with the first taste of dirt back in March, before the first hard spring rain.

Much like Moses, Africans and African Americans responded creatively and effectively to their agroecological dilemmas—curbing erosion, rotating crops, and terracing—through preservation-conservation, all the while navigating a labyrinth of racism and race as enslaved people and even as sharecroppers. They practiced a unique form of environmentalism that combined conservation and agricultural methods practiced before any African had yet set foot on the continent of North America.[20]

More recently, a group of African American farmers forming the Southeastern African-American Farmers Organic Network (SAA-FON) has been practicing and advocating organic farming, much like Moses. In states like Georgia and Louisiana, these farmers have turned to organic methods, such as foregoing chemical fertilizers and instead fertilizing with compost.

7

Children

DREAMING AND DANGER
IN WOODS AND FIELDS

In 1940, two Negro adults lead eight youths across the border from Louisiana into Mississippi for a field trip. They walk on a path trodden and weathered by feet, wind, and rain, traveling on a decline lit by the bright June sun through the understory of the trees. One youth, Roger Samford, is a bit older than the rest at sixteen. He draws on what he learned last year on the trail. Dustin signals his fourteen-year-old friend, pointing to an imperial moth. Picking it up for closer inspection, the boys discover the purple and yellow hue typical of the male. The boys' foreheads, covered in perspiration, touch as they lean in to observe the details of the antennae and fore- and hind wings. Together they list the moth's sources of food—sweet gum, pine, maple, oak, box elder, and sassafras—remembering yesterday's lesson back at the camp. Their mutual reverie is interrupted by silence; they no longer hear the voices of the others. After a moment of panic, the boys realize the path is clear before them, and they race ahead, catching their small band where the narrow waterfalls spill down a sheer brown wall of soil, rock, and moss traced with tree roots.

African American children, like these imagined boys exploring the woods on a field trip, also often worked in the fields. W. E. B. DuBois described in a romantic fashion the African American child's dual perspective of preservation and conservation—the woods and the field—at the turn of the twentieth century:

> Back toward town we glided, past the straight and thread-like pines, past a dark tree-dotted pond where the air was heavy with a dead sweet perfume. White slender-legged curlews flitted by us, and the garnet blooms of the cotton looked gay against the green and purple stalks. A peasant girl was hoeing in the field, white turbaned and black-limbed.[1]

Wilderness was also part of this unique children's environmental experience. Like the adults before them, African American children went into the woods for both refuge and transformation, including ceremonies marking initiation into adulthood. For the enslaved, including children, wilderness and civilization overlapped. Wilderness comprised complex landscapes of woods, swamps, and farms as children, too, hunted for food to eat and skins to drape around their bodies for warmth, hid in dark and high places as runaways, searched for resources from medicinal plants, sought places to rest in the shade of trees, and cultivated crops in the fields. The environment was both utilitarian and appealing. The wilderness of the swamp and the civilization of the tamed fields were interconnected for African Americans.[2]

From Africa to the American South, children were often treated as work hands—not as beloved and cherished beings—by the slaveholders in the fields. In addition, the family economy of sharecropping required that children work in the fields rather than attend school or play with their friends. From infancy, some children were cradled in rough slings in trees, and toddlers were left to their own devices on the edges of fields, unless elderly enslaved women, unable to manage heavy field or domestic work, cared for them in or near the quarters. These children watched from a distance as adults toiled over cotton, tobacco, sugarcane, and indigo. As enslaved children grew older, they ultimately worked in the heat and humidity, as did their parents. In adolescence, youth began harder labor as they stooped to pick cotton from prickly spines, reached to prime tobacco, and learned to pluck worms from the plants. In freedom, they suffered the same fate under the gaze of their parents in sharecropping, which often required the labor of the entire family.

Gender defined much of the children's labor even early on. Gangs of enslaved boys had a variety of tasks in agriculture. They collected manure from barns, later scattering it in fields. The boys raked the yards and barns, helped to cultivate gardens, and "watered trees, shelled corn, dug potatoes, picked peaches, gathered turkey manure, stacked wood, shucked corn for the hogs, and thinned corn by hand." Girls were generally exempt from gangs; instead they were forced to do domestic work or sent to the cotton fields at a young age because they were more nimble and efficient than boys at plucking the bolls, at least until around age sixteen, when the older boys and men generally outpaced the children and the women.[3]

Children who cultivated crops in the fields also experienced the practical and the whimsical in the environment. Mrs. Georgina Gibbs, who was born enslaved in 1849 in Portsmouth, Virginia, said this about the relationship between conservation and hard work during her childhood: "Work began at sun rise and last 'till sun down. When I wuz eight years old, I started working in de field wif two paddles to keep de crows from eatin' de crops." Nancy Williams of Norfolk, Virginia, shared a similar experience with a dose of abuse by the slaveholder:

> Guess I was a girl 'bout five or six when I was put wid de other chillum pickin' de bugs off de terbaccy leaves. Gal named Crissy was wukin' on nex' row, an' kep' whisperin' to me to pick 'em all off. Didn' pay no 'tention to her, any dat fell off jus' let lay dere. Purty soon old Masser come long, dough, an' see dat I done been missin' some of dem terbaccy worms. Picked up a hand full of worms, he did, anb' stuffed 'em inter my mouth; Lordy knows how many of dem shiny things I done swallered, but I sho' picked 'em off careful arter dat.

Children also protected crops against pests by serving as "human scarecrows," making all manner of noise to keep the birds from the fields. Even in freedom, sharecropper Ned Cobb induced his children to pluck boll weevils from the cotton: "I've gived my children many pennies and nickels for pickin' up squares. But fact of the business, pickin' up squares and burnin' 'em—it weren't worth nothin'." Cobb tried to use an organic method to remove pests through the labor of his children in an effort to avoid spreading poisonous arsenic.[4]

Enslaved children experienced nature in the woods by hunting, fishing, foraging, and playing beyond farm borders. They treated nature as a plaything, although slaveholders brutally exploited enslaved children, and as sharecroppers, parents were often forced to send their offspring to the fields. Lizzie Davis was one such enslaved child in South Carolina, amusing herself in the woods:

> Oh, we chillum would have de most fun dere ever was romanc- ing (roaming) dem woods in dat day en time. I used to think

Skills and hard labor of African Americans fueled the turpentine industry around the turn of the century.

Black Seminoles Scouts, circa 1913–14, descendants of enslaved Africans from Georgia and South Carolina who escaped to Florida. There, they lived among and had children with the Seminoles, who taught them scouting techniques.

An African American couple enjoying the woods.

Young children pulling cans to be recycled, Chicago YMCA Clean-up Campaign, 1919.

Stereoscope photograph of oyster and fish
women, Charleston, South Carolina, 1870.

Booker T. Washington, president
of Tuskegee Institute, circa 1911.

Booker T. Washington supervising sweet potato cultivation
at the Tuskegee Institute, circa 1916.

African American 4-H Club members displaying their cows in the middle of a baseball field, 1955.

Girl Scouts, circa 1955. The first African American Girl Scout troop was founded in 1917.

North Carolina Boy Scouts, 1958.

Damaged tobacco crop after
a hailstorm, circa 1963.

A young Southern child,
completely at ease in the
natural environment,
circa 1960.

George Washington Carver
(front row, center) with his
staff at the Tuskegee
Institute, 1902.

Children learning about corn and cotton at the Annie Davis School near Tuskegee, Alabama, 1902.

Booker T. Washington feeding chickens with food he raised on his own garden.

A nature study class in a rural black school, 1902.

A Tuskegee Institute out-
door nature study class.

Whittier School instruc-
tors and young students
on a field trip, Hampton,
Virginia, 1899.

Virginia farmer working
his land near Washington,
Virginia, 1940.

Booker T. Washington teaching a boy about
real country life.

Children picking cotton.

it was de nicest thing dat I been know 'bout to go down in de
woods side one of dem shady branch en get a cup of right cool
water to drink out de stream. I tell you, I thought dat was de
sweetest water I is ever swallowed.

She and the other children made a game of accessorizing their
clothes, often just rough shirts supplied by the slaveholders, complemented by nothing more than bare feet:

Den we chillum used to go out in de woods wid de crowd
en get in dese big oak leaves en hickory leaves en make hats.
Would use dese here long pine needles en thorns for de pins
dat we would pick up somewhe' dere in de woods. En we
would dress de hats wid all kind of wild flowers en moss dat
we been find scatter bout in de woods.

The children's game of dress-up was a curious counterpoint to
the fight launched by white women to save the plumed birds whose
feathers were plucked for the fashionable hats of the day.[5]
Continuing into the early twentieth century, African American teachers taught nature study to children, as depicted in photographs from the period. In one a teacher stands in front of
a classroom filled with schoolchildren. She has placed a small
evergreen—a pine—atop a table that she uses as a teaching tool.
In the background, she has written on the blackboard, "What do
we get from the pine?" and "The Pine: Size Parts." On another
occasion and in another photograph, Booker T. Washington, the
most renowned president of Tuskegee Institute, dressed in a suit
and a hat, bends to his knees with a young boy to his left and a
pine tree between them. The boy looks on, his hand on the tree,
and watches as Washington gathers what look to be leaves and
pine needles.

In another example, African American youth and young adults in an outdoor class line up carefully in their best attire near what appears to be an oak tree in the foreground, set among three or so other trees. Some grasp textbooks, nature guides, or notebooks in their hands; others clasp leaves; two young men measure the width of a tree trunk; and finally one youth perches atop a box as he reaches up to the leaves and limbs of an oak.

In yet another image, small children stand together in two groups: as one child touches a horse's leg, another holds the bridle, and one leans into its shoulder. In a final photograph, the African American Whittier School in Hampton, Virginia, takes its young students on a field trip. Three instructors dressed in long dresses and hats in the Victorian style stand along the perimeter of a group of twelve young children, all in their Sunday photo-ready best. One instructor gestures with her hands raised to waist level as she describes the locale. The group stands near water-loving trees, with a clump of black willows in the background. In the foreground are rushes, which place them on the edge of a stream or even the Chesapeake Bay or Hampton Roads Bay, all fed by the James River.

These snapshots of nature study classes and field trips show how nature was multifaceted for African Americans. They embraced the appeal of nature, always mindful that the practical implications of tapping turpentine, cutting down lumber from the forests, and harnessing animals like horses and cows on the farm were foremost.[6]

Negro 4-H Wildlife Conservation Conferences, a strand of the national 4-H clubs, blended conservation and preservation. Organizers launched clubs in Ohio and arranged corn contests in Illinois beginning in 1905, with other states in the Midwest quickly reproducing these efforts. The 4-H also mirrored the clubs devised for adults by the agricultural agencies of the Federal Extension Service through the Cooperative Extension Service and Home Demonstration Work, today the United States Department of Agriculture

(USDA). The Cooperative Extension Service modeled agricultural techniques for farmers to help restore the land by planting cover crops and preventing water and wind erosion. Home Demonstration Work trained women in canning, gardening, housekeeping, and sewing. These farmers and homemakers—legions of parents, uncles, aunts, and neighbors—were also exposed to the influences of children schooled in 4-H.

Local and federal efforts coalesced into the 4-H clubs, one of many government agricultural agencies launched through the 1914 Smith-Lever Act, the federal legislation that was the genesis of the USDA. In 1923, the Negro 4-H program reached its peak with 3,001 clubs numbering 21,893 boys and 34,078 girls, ranging in age from ten to nineteen. The youth participated in informal schooling, where they practiced what they learned in the fields and at home.

A 4-H club was launched in Missouri in 1907—with many other clubs that followed—rewarding junior leaders with camp outings. In 1922 the West Virginia 4-H arranged a camp in Denmar, and in 1924, North Carolina 4-H leaders organized camps in several cities and established coursework at a Greensboro college. Other Southern states' Negro 4-H clubs soon followed suit. In 1948 the first regional camp for "outstanding Negro boys and girls" was held at Southern University in Baton Rouge, Louisiana, with discussions about problems faced by the youth, presentations on agriculture, an outing to New Orleans, a boat trip on the Mississippi River, and a tour of Baton Rouge itself, the state capital.[7]

The Camp Whispering Pines 4-H Wildlife Conservation Conferences were held during the summers and included three to six days of class sessions and field trips. In North Carolina, the camps were located in Cary beginning in 1934 and later moved to Hammocks Beach, Swansboro, in 1956. Both were recreational demonstration areas from the 1930s to the 1960s. The conference existed after Theodore Roosevelt's Progressive period, yet Progressive ideals persisted, including an emphasis on the early environmentalism of conservation and preservation. The 4-H Wildlife Conservation Conferences modeled wildlife conservation for rural African American children and youth. Conference organizers and leaders encouraged and trained these future farmers to remain on the land, while teaching and modeling land conservation and agricultural techniques. The conferences also promoted the study of wild animals and birds. They undergirded rural economies in the United States, combining service and leisure activities with the goal of translating the work into expertise and labor for the further development of the rural South. Within the milieu of debates about conservation versus preservation that polarized the white, mainstream environmental movement across the nation, the Negro 4-H camps entwined two environmental ideologies of utility and appreciation typical of rural life. Contradictions were served to the youth in a mélange of farming, hunting, nature classes, and field trips.[8]

The 4-H symbol embodied the goals of the conferences. On a 1940 program cover from North Carolina, the national emblem of a four-leaf clover—a drawing probably rendered by a child—links the Hs to four images: a flying bird; a copse of trees; a creek bordered by a farm, bushes, and trees; and a butterfly. Both nationally and locally, the 4-H clubs and the conferences unified the competing themes of profit, service, and leisure in conservation and nature study with the foundational Hs of head, heart, hands, and health:

I pledge
my Head to clearer thinking
my Heart to greater loyalty
my Hands to larger service and
my Health to better living
For my club, my community, and my country.

Although the image on the conference cover was in black and white, a color version of the symbol reveals green representing nature and white signifying purity.[9]

The leaders taught and modeled conservation coursework in the areas of soil, insects, forestry, and hunting: Soil Conservation was critical to farming and forestry; Insects and Conservation focused on insect or pest control in places like fields, gardens, and orchards, so important in sustaining the rural Southern economy; Forestry and Conservation included a field trip and sessions on tree identification, which complemented other classes on the damaging effects of deforestation and the solution of planting seedlings, a form of conservation; and finally, Game and Fur-Bearing Animals—Field Trip emphasized hunting game to put meat on the table and supply skins for coats, hats, shoes, and gloves.[10]

The Negro 4-H conferences used the word *preserve* but in essence practiced conservation to guarantee game for hunting in the future. Conversely, nature study was closer to the traditional meaning of preservation, taught through lessons, arts and crafts, and field trips. Very broadly, nature study classes took a holistic view, focusing, as a 1945 camp program stated, "on the resources about us in nature and our everyday lives to learn more of the life about us and how the stones, the soil, plants, and animals work and can be made to add to our comfort and pleasure."[11]

One of the first activities on most schedules over the years was a field trip: Identification of Wild Flowers and Shrubs and Their Use in Beautification. It promised to help youth to "become better acquainted with our native flowers and shrubs. Practical work in beautifying will also be held." The next day, campers went on the Bird Identification Tour, learning "the calls of birds, identifying marks of birds," while discussing "the breeding and feeding habits of birds in the area." These field trips were commonplace throughout the years of the conferences. The themes—soil, insects, forestry, hunting, and nature study—were brought together in Arts and Crafts—The Making of a Scrap-book for Wildlife Conservation Project, a hybrid course that blended conservation and preservation.[12]

From conservation to forestry to hunting to nature study, African American leaders in the 4-H created spaces for youth to breathe fresh air and hike through the woods. The intricate relationships built on money, influence, race relations, and community reverberated when the children sang "America," known for phrases like "land where my fathers died," "I love thy rocks and rills / thy woods and templed hills," "let music swell the breeze / and ring thru all the trees," "let rocks their silence break," and "long may our land be bright / with freedom's holy light." The fathers referred to in the song's lyrics were the architects for white freedom after the American Revolution, and the concept of freedom for whites was reinforced through colonial and antebellum enslavement. Yet African American children also sang this anthem, which was filled with environmental references, and expressed their own patriotism and allegiance to America, rooted in what it meant to be black in America. Such patriotism was also evident in the image of an American eagle in its nest on the cover of a conference program.[13]

In her autobiography Zora Neale Hurston described the whimsy of nature in rural Eatonville, Florida, an African American town, around 1904, when she was a young teenager. Her images provide some context for the camps:

> The wind would sough through the tops of the tall, long-leaf pines and said things to me. I put in the words the sounds put in me. Like "woo woo, you woo!" The tree was talking to me, even when I did not catch the words. It was talking and telling me things. I have mentioned the tree, near our house that got so friendly I named it "the loving pine." Finally all my

playmates called it that too. I used to take a seat at the foot of that tree and play for hours without any other toys. We talked about everything in my world. Sometimes we just took it out in singing songs. That tree had a might fine bass voice when it really took a notion to let it out.

Hurston expressed her love for the wind and her favorite tree in this excerpt and made nature human in both her fiction and non-fiction over the years. Here the tree, a friend, spoke to her as she romped with her playmates and sang to her when she was alone. Like other African American children she found solace as she played in nature. Although the reality and backdrop of African American life were hard labor and inequity, African Americans found ways to take comfort in nature and make it their own.[14]

The same was true for children who were enslaved or worked in sharecropping families, who experienced nature in practical and whimsical ways that continued with the Negro 4-H conferences from the 1930s into the 1960s. Rural African Americans in the South had no choice but to stress the practical side of conservation for the sake of their livelihoods, while blending recreation and preservation in the conferences.

8

Nature Study

OBSERVING, CLASSIFYING, AND UTILIZING THE NATURAL WORLD

In a meadow bounded by a copse of oaks and a stream, Anabel, a young woman, sits in the grass in the warm morning sun as she plans a field trip, an assignment for her class Nature Study for Teachers, at a Negro college in North Carolina. She remembers her ancestor Yooku, an African priest who gathered herbs from the land, and her grandparents Albert and Marie, who worked the fields in Louisiana. It seems to Anabel that her family's connection with the land has come full circle as she learns about ways to teach about nature.

Mentally returning to her surroundings, Anabel watches a swallowtail—a gray butterfly spotted with blue, white, and orange—float onto her papers. She hears the cadence of a cardinal not far away. She writes notes in measured, unfurling strokes in her notebook, careful not to brush the butterfly away. She shifts position to stretch out on her blanket and sees a blue jay with blue-black and white coloring perched on the limb of an oak tree. Squirrels hasten across the ground and leap along the limbs of the trees. The young woman's eyes drift to the clear, running stream set against the blue sky touched with white-gray clouds. She listens to the splash of water against the stream's bed and rocks.

Pulling herself off the blanket, Anabel walks toward the water and spots striped bass swimming past an abandoned and crumbling beaver dam. The sky darkens—perhaps it is going to rain. She moves back to her blanket, papers, and scraps, stoops to collect them and then walks quickly toward the school before the rain descends. Back at the dorm, she finishes the assignment, readying the presentation that she has already staged in the meadow and will deliver to the instructor and her fellow students Monday morning.

Anabel's story emerges from a history of nature study and wildlife conservation that formed part of the rural curriculum at African American teacher-training schools, secondary schools, and agricultural colleges like Hampton Institute in Virginia. These institutions trained future farmers, school administrators, government agents, and teachers in agriculture, complemented by a nature study curriculum. Instructors and teachers taught and modeled preservation by observing and classifying plants, animals, and insects in nature and in the classroom. Nature study and wildlife conservation were two strands brought together in rural preservation-conservation.

In part, this curriculum was adapted from Cornell University's Nature Study School, which opened in 1897 and developed into a national environmental movement introduced and then spread by whites through turn-of-the-century reform. Nature study responded to the ills of industrialization, such as poverty, inferior housing, disease, and corporate vice, which social reformers wanted to eradicate. Though their emphasis was on the big city, reformers worked in rural places, including parts of the South. Some encouraged Southerners, including African Americans, to study and teach practical preservation in the form of nature study with rural children, part of a national rather than local reform effort.

Nature study was designed to encourage rural people to stay on and appreciate farms and their surrounding environs of woods, swamps, rivers, and fields rather than move to towns and cities. Unlike in the North, where whites generally populated rural communities and worked the land, as in the region surrounding Cornell in Ithaca, African Americans were the blood, bones, and gristle of agricultural labor in the South. African American administrators in Southern education joined together preservation-conservation, appreciation, and exploitation, to stabilize the African American workforce that supported the white, Southern way of life. African American teachers shared the beauty of nature in the midst of the routine and monotony of rising early, tending to livestock, repairing buildings and fences, and cultivating farmland.

African Americans developed their own nature study programs in tandem with a national movement that was characterized by a curriculum developed in white schools. Continuing into the twentieth century, that mainstream movement was largely rooted in the theological and the aesthetic. The study of nature was seen as morally and spiritually beneficial, although the science of nature study was gradually given more emphasis.[1]

Anna Comstock furthered the nature study curriculum as an instructor at Cornell, publishing a guidebook favored by secondary school teachers. Her calling began in the school of agriculture at Cornell, where she taught her first nature study course in 1899 to urban students. Comstock spent two days per week lecturing, leading students on field trips, and doing lab work. When she taught the class for a second time in 1900, her audience shifted to country teachers in normal or elementary schools surrounding Cornell, as originally mandated by the university's nature study curriculum. She retired in 1921. In the midst of teaching, she published her *Handbook of Nature Study* (1911). The nature bible, as it came to be called, became a Cornell University Press bestseller and inspired many teachers in the field.[2]

In addition to using Comstock's *Handbook of Nature Study*, schools also modeled their work on John H. Gehrs's *Agricultural Nature Study* (1929). A section titled "How to Attract and Protect Birds" reads: "Half the joy of the springtime would be missing if we did not have the gay colors and merry songs of the birds to warn us that summer is coming. In summer as well as winter we may easily attract the birds to our homes if we supply the necessary conditions."

In his book Gehrs makes some general recommendations for teaching this lesson in elementary schools:

We may (1) provide artificial nesting places for them, (2) protect their natural nesting places, such as the trees and shrubbery, (3) protect wild fruit-bearing trees and shrubs, or plant sunflowers and other seed-bearing plants, so that the birds will always be supplied with food, (4) form bird clubs to study the habits of birds, and (5) study the game law and find how we can help the government protect and encourage birds.[3]

African Americans taught and practiced preservation in colleges and secondary schools like Tuskegee Institute and Hampton Institute—marginalized schools in marginalized places that offered African Americans educations and maintained the racial caste system in the South that benefited whites. Although ostensibly contradicting more pragmatic methods of conservation in farmer training, the schools modeled how to appreciate trees and animals. Rural teachers taught nature study to encourage children to stay on the farms, the agenda of the national movement, particularly in the South.[4]

Such a model was reinforced in Mary Alice Armstrong's 1902 *Southern Workman* review of *Nature Study and Life* (1902), a textbook by Clifton H. Hodge. The African American readership of the Hampton publication was exposed to the textbook, which was one of the first books to be incorporated into this secondary school curriculum and become critical to the nature study movement. Armstrong wrote, "One practical result of this method of nature should be to surround our homes and schoolhouses with the most beautiful thing attainable. It should instill the spirit of creating and preserving the natural beauties of roadside and field and forest rather than that of ruthless destruction."[5]

Hampton Institute further integrated nature study into its teacher training curriculum. On letterhead emblazoned with "Hampton Normal and Agricultural Institute—Nature Study Bureau," the school outlined a practical course of study: "The work in Nature Study, while broad, will be technical enough to develop the highest grade of mental power and will lay the foundation for the work in agriculture." Hampton lauded nature study, comparing it to Latin or chemistry, and attempted to satisfy the more professional desires and goals of future teachers and extension agents. A 1903 letter from Hampton to the Board of Education of the District of Columbia reported on one class:

> The common forms of plant and animal life were examined, half of the time being given to each branch. All facts were obtained from living growing specimens and not text books. The subjects most likely to interest children, the wise selection of important points and the best methods of presentation were discussed. Model lessons with classes from the Practice School to show the application of method in the school room were frequently given.

Hampton Institute offered two other classes: Birding (bird watching) and Drawing, in which students sketched the inanimate and animate in nature—both means of expressing nature appreciation. Teachers shared this knowledge with young children. In addition, the instructors and students identified and studied trees through fieldwork.[6]

Hampton Institute published literature to assist the teacher with nature study in her classroom. One Hampton leaflet, *Course in Nature Study for Primary Grades*, described many areas in which to develop a curriculum for the classroom. A course called Garden Work entailed planting bulbs, nurturing plants and flowers, and identifying different parts of those plants and flowers. Children could identify and describe the parts of trees, such as the tulip tree. They could also learn about fruits, including apples and persimmons: "[E]ach fruit should be outlined according to form, contents, relation of parts, mode of disseminating seed, and usefulness to man and animals." Insects, including the destructive cabbage caterpillar, along with animals—rabbits, squirrels, birds, turtles, slugs, snails, mice, and earthworms—were to be observed and cataloged through the guidance of the teacher. Domesticated farm animals—the dog, cat, horse, cow, sheep, and hen—were given equal time, as they were part of a landscape that connected the farm with the woods, lakes, creeks, and rivers.[7]

The leaflet also outlined curricula to be taught out in the woods:

> Ask the children by what other name the pine leaves are known. Why? Would this name be appropriate for other evergreen leaves? Why?
>> If Mother Nature patches
>> The leaves of the trees and vines,
>> I'm sure she does her darning
>> With the needles of the pines.

The lesson also suggested encouraging children to bring a variety of needles and pine cones to class. Teachers were told to "Ask on what trees they found them. Ask what they might call such trees. What is the difference between old and fresh cones?" From smaller to larger, the pine tree was to be studied for "shape, height, bark, arrangement of branches, and angle they make with the trunk." And since nature was a practical means to an end, the leaflet advised that "the standing trees are useful in breaking the force of the wind; they also give beauty to a landscape. The stumps could be used for fences." But more important, the pine yielded turpentine, rosin, and tar—practical returns.[8]

Tuskegee Institute also had its own nature study program. Its literature noted:

> The purpose of the work in Nature Study is to train the power of observation, create an interest in and love for nature, increase knowledge which will be of service in the future and to cultivate an interest in agriculture. . . . The subject matter of this course, being divided into four groups, is so arranged with regard to the seasons of the year and for the facility of study. The purpose of this study is to create in students both an aesthetic and scientific appreciation for Nature, as well as to encourage an active rather than a passive attitude towards the things in Nature with which they come in contact daily.

In the fall, the students were to take up "general plant study," later in the semester studying the "seasonal changes and distribution of plants and animals over the earth's surface." During the second term or the winter, they were to complete "a general study of animals," along with "a study of seeds and flowers."[9]

Outside the walls of Hampton and Tuskegee, the powerhouses in African American education of the day, other schools also encouraged nature study. The *Bulletin of the Florida Agricultural and Mechani-*

cal College for Negroes suggested that teachers in rural schools in Florida lead children to beautify the grounds of their schools. In addition, children were to be shown "how to have little box gardens or pot gardens on small tables, boxes or shelves at the classroom window," filled with many plants and flowers, including begonias, roses, ferns, lantana, phlox, and marigolds. Diverse vegetables also filled those window sills: mustard, cabbage, and sweet potatoes, to name a few. Alternately, the teachers were urged to tell their students to "borrow from the neighbors, especially from the farm homes, or buy cheaply from private families, or use those you had raised yourself." The children were to be introduced to organic methods to rid plants of pests: "If large insects bother the plants, pick them off with the fingers, or by some means and destroy them. If menaced by very small insects, especially the tiny brown scale, plant lice, etc., wash the parts carefully with a soft cloth dipped in strong soap suds, but don't break off young leaf buds."[10]

Mrs. Ester B. Fountain, a teacher at the African American Slater Winston-Salem summer secondary school in North Carolina, taught a class called Methods of Nature Study. Students identified yard- and wildflowers, trees, birds, and insects and traced the extinction of wildflowers. Students hiked, presented exhibits, and picked, mounted, and pressed flowers. Fountain shared similar activities with students, using trees to identify "the fruits and seeds of shade trees," pine, juniper, and coconut. They classified "seeds that fly away; seeds that swim; seeds that coast; and seeds that steal a ride." The class also cared for wounded birds, built birdhouses and feeding pens, listened to and identified bird songs, and studied their habits. What is more, the children examined the uses of, the effects on, and the structure of insects, including "moths, butterflies, flies, grass-hoppers, wasps, [and] caterpillars."[11] They collected and mounted flowers and insects for display while capturing and distinguishing the eating habits of insects. In 1919 the teachers at the African American St. Augustine School in North Carolina taught similar lessons to a fifth-grade class. These schools concentrated on identifying flora and fauna, hiking, and caring for sickly creatures in preservationist nature study activities.

Schools used some of the same nature texts found in the Hampton Institute course titled Nature Study, with themes focusing on birding, waterways, animals, flowers, trees, and plants: Keeler's *Our Native Trees and How to Identify Them*; Merriam's *Birds of Village and Field*; Wilson's *Nature Study*; Mrs. Miller's *Brook Book*; Cooper's *Animal Life in the Sea and on the Land*; Burrough's *Squir els* [sic] *and Other Fur Bearers*; and Hodge's *Nature Study and Life*. Other titles included Bailey's *Botany*, Bailey's *The Principles of Agriculture*, Bailey's *Gardenmaking*, Comstock's *Insect Life*, Dana's *How to Know Wild Flowers*, and Dana's *Plants and Their Children*.[12]

Africans in America were forced and coerced to cultivate the land without remuneration and with little or no autonomy. As a result, many eschewed agricultural labor. Yet they still understood nature, more than many whites, because they had their hands in the soil, their eyes on the sky, and their ears attuned to the flutter of butterflies. African Americans were immersed in nature. One such woman from enslavement was Gloria Naylor's character Sapphira Wade, a conjure woman who was enslaved and born in 1799 in Willow Springs, an island off the North Carolina and Georgia coasts. In her modern novel *Mama Day* (1998), Naylor shows the intricacies of the relationship between people of African descent and nature, long before the teaching of a nature study curriculum. Sapphira

could walk through a lightning storm without being touched; grab a bolt of lightning in the palm of her hand; use the heat of lightning to start kindling going under her medicine pot; depending upon which of us takes to mind her. She turned the moon into salve, the stars into a swaddling cloth, and healed wounds of every creature walking up on two or down on four.

Whatever was in that medicine pot came from the woods or perhaps Sapphira's own garden; whatever healed people and livestock was for practical use. At the same time, her aesthetic expression came through in the description of lightning, the moon, and the stars in nature.[13]

Nature study was much the same, as African American schools with limited resources fostered an appreciation of nature in the context of farming—a practical preservation like Sapphira's in *Mama Day.* Instructors could find tools in schools and leaflets to guide young children to classify wildflowers, save birds with broken wings, or hike through the hills and mountains of the South. Teachers and students could appreciate two very different aspects of agricultural or rural environmentalism in agricultural education and nature study. Although ostensibly contradicting conservation, in a setting where rural African Americans worked hard to produce crops and make profits, teachers and children had the opportunity to practice and revel in a preservationist's appreciation of nature. African Americans did all this at schools limited by racism. They sent students-turned-teachers off to teach small children at segregated schools where they were probably limited by the plants and patches of land available to them.

The good work continues. In 2009 the First Lady of the United States, Michelle Obama, took up the mantle of those dedicated teachers and cultivated a vegetable garden on the grounds of the White House. She used the garden to feed her own family but also invited schoolchildren to the garden to learn about sustainability.

9

Women and Gardening

A PATCH OF HER OWN

To plant her flower and vegetable garden, Lola Lampre, an African American woman and great-great grandchild of Minkah, uses her darkly creviced and freckled hands, her broad, strong shoulders and back, and her wiry, muscled arms. She drops small seeds into the soil and manages to compost hay, manure, and field stubble after transplanting bushes from the woods earlier that day in her yard. She cuts several sunflowers from the garden in the back as the sun seems to move in and out behind the drifting clouds. She takes the path from the garden to the house and walks into her kitchen. With her strong arms, she grasps the freshly cut flowers she'll use to decorate the kitchen table in her home, adding color for when her husband, Edgar, and their three sons come in from the fields for a meal that will include string beans, potatoes, and melon from the garden.

Lola and her family reflect a unique environmental perspective among some Southern African American women by way of the gardens they tended as first enslaved and then free women. One such woman was the writer Alice Walker's mother, who greatly influenced her daughter. In her nonfiction collection *In Search of Our Mothers' Gardens*, Walker writes, "Guided by my heritage of a love of beauty and a respect for strength—in search of my mother's garden, I found my own."[1] African Americans continued these practices and held these perspectives into the twentieth century.

Gardening was one example of preservation and conservation blending in the rural Southern setting for African American women. They cultivated with simple tools: a hoe, trowel, or shovel in one hand and seeds or fertilizer in the other. African American women developed expertise from both community knowledge and their own interpretations of agricultural methods. Rural African American women and men often supported one another in complementary roles and with strategies designed to support the family unit. These women harvested vegetables for meals and planted shrubs and cultivated flowers for more appealing homes. Despite the limitations imposed by enslavement, sharecropping, and racism, including limited access to better land, agricultural methods, and plants or crops, these women took some patches and attempted to make them their own through aesthetics and conservation efforts.

African American women and society defined their roles in the separate spheres for men and women that were commonplace in Victorian America and beyond. But the African American community valued the productivity of women, which reinforced a commitment to work in the home and garden. Enslaved and free women were not passive and proper Victorian women at home and work. Whether accepting or rejecting Victorian mores, African American men and women worked together in complementary roles as part of a viable economic strategy to better conditions for their families.[2]

Some ridiculed the value of the women's contributions to household productivity and demonstrated enormous condescension in their efforts to uplift the poor. Thomas Monroe Campbell criticized rural African American women as "too careless as to the loud manner in which they act in the streets and in public places . . . and unduly familiar with men."[3]

Such an indictment coming out of an African American man's mouth may have simply parroted the greater society's views concerning these women. But, ultimately, African American women in the rural South controlled how and where they gardened and, by implication, why they gardened.

It is unclear whether gardens by African Americans were more "African" or "American" in nature. Perhaps further study in gardening will reveal more.[4] African Americans practiced two types of gardening—one that mimicked nature and another that imposed order through the row system. With the first type, gardeners reinforced African traditions as the enslaved, sharecroppers, and even members of gardening clubs created distinctively African American spaces that simultaneously mimicked nature and rejected white control. Although the gardens appeared chaotic, the disarray of plants also created a diversity that reduced opportunities for weeds and pests to take hold. Some gardeners sought ethical, moral, and spiritual enlightenment in these chaotic or wilderness spaces much as their African ancestors had.[5]

In her short story "The Gilded Six-Bits," published in 1933, Zora Neale Hurston fictionalized just such an early twentieth-century yard cared for by a character named Missy May. "The front yard was parted in the middle by a sidewalk from gate to door-step, a sidewalk edged on either side by quart bottles driven neck down into the ground on a slant. A mess of homey flowers planted without a plan but blooming cheerily from their helter-skelter place."

In the 1912 novel *The "Passin'-On" Party*, the white writer Effie Graham depicted an urban African American woman in turn-of-the-twentieth-century Kansas who kept "a half-pleasing, half-offending jumble of greenery and gleaming color, of bush and vine; of vegetable and blooming flower; of kitchen ware, crockery, and defunct household furniture." Graham disparagingly compared the yard to an African jungle, park, and dump.[6]

Yet other African Americans planted symmetrical gardens that likely were rooted in row-crop traditions. They valued doing things properly by applying a "right way" for arranging and planting. Neighbors often competed in a friendly fashion, also doing it the "right way," using a uniform design, aesthetics, and old-fashioned labor.[7]

These gardens, whether cultivated in seeming chaos or the row system, were distinct from those planted by white women. Both groups designed and maintained yards and gardens that included flowers, shrubs, trees, and plants purchased individually, accepted as gifts, or cultivated from cuttings. African Americans, however, were more likely to create colorful motifs from gifts and castoffs. African American traditions were so ingrained that plants presented as gifts were associated with the giver.[8]

African American women manipulated and controlled their yards for multiple functions. Free-range areas, or pens, in which livestock could roam; extended kitchens from their houses; spaces for cleaning and leisure; swept areas; pathways to the fields, woods, and slaveholders' houses; and fenced flower and vegetable gardens created overlapping spaces in their yards. Each function, each space, was often fluid, with few or no boundaries. Unlike most enslaved people, African American renters and owner-operators had some income and could purchase livestock, including chickens and hogs, which were given free rein of the yard. Women sought the shade and protection of trees to prepare meals, feed and entertain family and friends, scrape pots, scrub dishes, wipe tables, beat rugs, and launder clothing. Children played, and adults sought recreation throughout their yards, particularly in the shade. Outside the green areas, women carefully swept clean any foliage or weeds, creating bare and austere spaces. The pathways took the women beyond their homes and yards to the environs of the woods, fields, big houses, neighboring plantations and farms, and towns.[9]

In these gardens African American women planted vegetables, fruits, flowers, shrubs, trees, and plants in red clay, sandy, and dark loamy soils. They generally cultivated vegetable gardens on the sides or at the backs of their cabins for easy access. To keep out livestock, their partners built enclosures of tied stakes for gardens. Most women grew vegetables primarily to sustain their families. They planted okra, milo, eggplant, collards, watermelon, white yams, peas, tomatoes, beans, squash, red peppers, onions, cabbage, potatoes, and sweet potatoes. Others planted truck gardens and sold corn, cotton, peanuts, sweet potatoes, tobacco, indigo, watermelons, and gourds at the market for profit. They also grew flowers for everyone's viewing and pleasure, beckoning neighbors to look closer or visitors to chat in the yard's fragrance and color. The women looked out on exquisite flowers, including petunias, buttercups, verbenas, day lilies, cannas, chrysanthemums, iris, and phlox planted in the ground and in old tires, bottles, planters, and tubs. They placed shrubs—roses, azaleas, altheas, forsythia, crepe myrtle, spirea, camellias, nandina, and wild honeysuckle—throughout the yard. Azaleas and roses were most commonly planted. The dogwood, oak, chestnut, pine, red maple, black locust, sassafras, hickory, willow, cottonwood, and redbud trees dotted the landscape. They chose ornamental plants that were self-propagating, along with annuals that were generally self-seeding. Colorful combinations of blues, reds, pinks, oranges,

whites, and yellows often clashed with little or no sequencing. Placement was generally informal, wherever the gardeners could find
space. A mix of color and placement resulted in a lack of symmetry
and formal design—perhaps of African origin. In addition, African
Americans simply could not afford to buy several shrubs, plants,
or flowers at the same time as would have been necessary to create
such symmetry.[10]

One of the enslaved vividly remembered the leafy plants and
bright blossoms encircling the family cabin: "Us live in a log house
wid a little porch in front and de mornin' glory vines use to climb
'bout it. When they bloom, de bees would come hummin' 'round and
suck the honey out de blue bells on the vines. I members dat well
'nough, dat was a pleasant memory."[11] Slaves transformed yards and
decorated houses to make their spaces their own, setting them apart
from those of the slaveholders.

Dating back to the antebellum period, enslaved people also used
organic methods such as composting, when they took or were given
the opportunity to grow their own gardens. They composted oak
leaves with fire ash and applied barnyard manure and human waste
to fertilize their gardens. Although African American men reinforced
gender roles during enslavement by cultivating the tiny household
garden plots allotted to families by slaveholders and tilling their own
vegetable plots when time allowed, enslaved women also contributed.
A Louisiana gardener, an enslaved man, also built birdhouses from
hollowed gourds to attract nesting birds that protected vegetables
from insects and other pests. The birdhouses (now a fixture in modern suburban backyards) provided shelter for the birds that served as
natural pest control.

Enslaved women either worked with men or were responsible
for the vegetable gardens planted primarily for family consump-
tion. Casper Rumple, an enslaved man in De Valls Bluff, Arkansas,

recounted how African American women cultivated the plantation garden for Miss Rebecca, the mistress of the plantation:

> Another thing women had to do was work in the garden. It was a three acre garden. . . . They had plenty stock and all the fertilizer needed in the garden and patches. They had goober patch, popcorn patch, sorghum patches, several of 'em, pea patches but they were field cabbage patch and watermelon patch.

Were direct decisions about the garden made by the enslaved women or the white mistress? It is doubtful that Miss Rebecca worked directly in the garden, particularly if she supervised enslaved women to do such demanding work, so ultimately decisions concerning the diversification of vegetables and the use of manure were probably left to the laborers.[12]

After emancipation, educated African American women sought to establish partnerships with men that served both the men's and the women's needs. Although women were subordinate, men and women complemented one another, and the women did their best to do their part. Similarly, rural African American women and men cooperated with one another, cultivating very loosely along gender lines. Generally men tended fields and women kept gardens unless the labor-intensive sharecropping economy required both women and children in the fields. African American men produced cash crops to support their families after enslavement was dismantled. Women expanded their roles by cultivating family vegetable patches and planting ornamental and flower gardens.

Gardens served as sources of food for women's families, means of enhancing their homes, and, in some circumstances, small sources of revenue. The women improved their families' nutrition with homegrown vegetables and saved money by limiting the use of store-bought goods. African American women supplemented their pantries with turnip and collard greens, staples in their gardens. The women also created visual appeal in the feminine domain with flowers and ornamental plants outside their homes.

This is not so say this gendered division of labor was never crossed. Out of necessity or desire, women and children worked in the fields, and men enjoyed gardening, as did women. For the women, though, the home and garden were often the focal points. As Mary C. Gates wrote in a 1901 issue of *Southern Workman*, "Order in a home, like the regularity of nature—her sunrise or sunset, her seed-time and harvest—gives rhythmical swing to life."[13]

African American women who gardened cultivated flower patches for visual appeal, as captured by folk artist Clementine Hunter. Her painting *These Big Vases, They Is Called Spanish Water Jars* (ca. 1940), an oil on paper, can be interpreted broadly as a larger-than-life flowering plant harnessed in a pot and dwarfing a woman and nature—a metaphor for overshadowing humankind. In more mundane terms, the woman next to the potted plant could be making a quick stop in the garden—with a hat on her head, her hair in a bun, wearing a dressy blouse and an ankle-length skirt and wrapped up in an apron as an afterthought—for a flower or two to complement the table.[14]

In *Calinda Corvier Was Over 100 Years Old* (ca. 1940), an oil painting on a window shade, Hunter explores the meaning of leisure and nature for an older woman and young child. Hunter paints another oversized flowering plant in a blue pitcher on a red table. Calinda is holding up a child, perhaps a granddaughter, head wrapped in a red bonnet; conceivably she cares for this child during the day, as those much younger and stronger work. Is it dusk? Is it a gray morning? In either case, Hunter depicts a built environment of shrubs, large red flowers, green grass, and a tall tree that surrounds and captures the woman and child in a static moment of leisure.[15]

Like Clementine Hunter, Alice Walker describes an aesthetic sensibility in gardening, as the author reminisces about her mother, who kept a flower garden in the 1930s and 1940s:

> I remember people coming to my mother's yard to be given cuttings from flowers; I hear again the praise showered on her because whatever rocky soil she landed on, she turned into a garden. A garden so brilliant with colors, so original in its design, so magnificent with life and creativity, that to this day people drive by our house in Georgia—perfect strangers and imperfect strangers—and ask to stand or walk among my mother's art. I notice that it is only when my mother is working in her flowers that she is radiant, almost to the point of being invisible—except as Creator: hand and eye. She is involved in work her soul must have. Ordering the universe in the image of her personal conception of Beauty.[16]

African American women practiced gardening through conservation techniques including transplanting, diversification, and fertilizing. They dug up woodland flowers to improve their cabins and transplanted azaleas, wild roses, honeysuckle, and dogwoods in their yards.

Many African Americans who grew up in the South in the mid-twentieth century can recall their mothers' gardens vividly. In Alabama, Onnie Lee Logan, a midwife, reminisced:

> We had three big gardens. String beans, butter beans, turnip greens, English peas, sweet potatoes, Irish potatoes, okra, ever'thing. Tomatoes, three or four different kinds of squash

> . . . love, care, and share, that's what we did. We had it and my
> daddy and mother they shared with the ones that didn't have
> it. Mother would send a piece and share.

Her mother's resourceful diversification of vegetables made good gardening sense, which translated into community and social responsibility that was common among rural African Americans.

Lacey Gray, from Longleaf, Louisiana, said that her mother fed her healthy food from the garden: "Mother never used pesticides or chemical fertilizers, and we never had problems with insects either. Used cow manure on big crops and chicken manure on the kitchen garden." Mary Lee from Shreveport, Louisiana, reminisced about her mother, who used laundry water—so-called gray water—to fertilize the vegetables and herbs in her yard.[17]

These preservation-conservation traditions in gardening and the values of the women who practiced them are mirrored in the novel *Camilla's Roses* (2004) by Bernice L. McFadden. This passage describes a rose bush in a garden:

> Almost perfect. It was the rosebush that caused the envy and
> thievery. Where it came from no one knew for sure. Algiers
> or Morocco, depending on who was telling the story. . . . Hor-
> ticulturalists came from all over the country to see this rose-
> bush that did not grow in any other part of the country and
> all of the attention elevated its owners up to a kind of celebrity
> status. It had been stolen a number of times, dug up in the
> thick of night and hauled away by some jealous neighbor; but
> always returned, wilted half-dead. . . . Back in its own soil, in
> its front-yard home again, the rosebush flourished and so did
> Abbey, coming up pregnant each time the rosebush was stolen
> and returned; she gave birth to ten children; eight girls and
> two boys, christening every one of the girls with the middle

name Rose. And they in turn did the same and the same holds true for every girl child after that and so on and so on.[18]

The rosebush carefully tended by Abbey, an African American woman, reflects the same care taken by African American women from enslavement to the early twentieth century in their own yards. In addition, two references bridge Africa with the United States: in the first the rose originates in Algiers or Morocco, and in the second McFadden makes reference to matrilineal naming of girls, a tradition of African origin. McFadden recounts the women's stories through plants stolen, lost, and retrieved. These portraits are so like the back stories of the African American women in history who planted flowers, some influenced as far back as Africa. At the same time the women struggle to keep their families—also stolen, lost, and retrieved, from their capture in Africa to enslavement and freedom in the United States—intact. McFadden uses the rose as part of a landscape to define Abbey and her children.

African American women like Abbey were the creative sources of gardening in their communities from enslavement to the twentieth century. By using yards, often in different ways than men, women took possession of them. They manipulated and interpreted the spaces for sustenance, comfort, joy, and sometimes profit.

These women—wives, mothers, sisters, and friends—continue to create such gardens. Vaughn Sills is a photographer who has been capturing traditional African American gardens in the South, belonging to women like Bea Robinson in Athens, Georgia, for more than fifteen years in a series called "Places for the Spirit." Sills says these entrancing gardens are "about the earth, about beauty, and about spirit."[19]

10

Environmental Justice

FREE TO BREATHE

When David Gibson, Anabel and Justin's son, was born in 1937, no one in the family in rural Louisiana could have imagined the civil rights movement, much less David helping to define the movement as a Baptist pastor in Louisiana. His ancestor Minkah, his great-great-granduncle and an African priest, seemed to call to David as he fought for equality for African Americans as a member of the Southern Christian Leadership Conference. David even stood below the Lincoln monument listening to Martin Luther King Jr.'s "I Have a Dream" speech after the peaceful march on Washington, D.C.

Many years later, in 2001, his experience in the civil rights movement became critical in Louisiana. The people in his little town in the shadow of a petrochemical company were in danger. The pollution from the processing plant had spewed pollutants, impacting the breathing of the elderly and the children more than anyone else in the community. Chemicals had also seeped into the soil and groundwater. Could there be a correlation between the poison in the sky, soil, and water and the unusually high rates of respiratory problems and cancer? At his church, David called together the members of the congregation and others in his town, forming an environmental advocacy group to organize a class-action lawsuit, lobby against big business in Washington, D.C., and care for his neighbors who had been debilitated by illnesses related to the environment.

Reflecting a historical experience similar to David's fictional struggle, people of color and the poor have long suffered in the United States as a result of the government and corporations dumping toxins and garbage into marginalized neighborhoods. Some African Americans have become activists, like David, who drew upon the civil rights movement to remedy these injustices.

This model of self-empowerment for environmental justice owes much to Martin Luther King Jr. In 1955, King, among others, transformed Rosa Parks's refusal to sit at the back of the bus into a church-based movement, igniting the mid-twentieth-century civil rights movement. Throughout his ministry of nonviolent activism, King defined social justice through a biblical lens, agitating for civil rights, condemning the Vietnam War, and in his final act before he was assassinated, advocating for sanitation workers. His historical legacy has endured and is now a cornerstone of the environmental justice movement.

More recently, in 1998 the *Christian Recorder* noted that "a new generation of Rosa Parks and Martin Luther Kings, Jrs. [sic] are meeting in churches to pray and plan and then heading out to work for the health of their communities."[1] This torch ignited once again in the wake of Hurricane Katrina in 2005, a modern-day instance of environmental inequity.

African American grassroots organizations launched the environmental justice movement to defend and advocate for contemporary African Americans exposed to toxins and pollution from landfills, garbage dumps, auto mechanic shops, and sewage plants.

Environmental justice scholars like Robert Bullard have documented that some in the public and private sectors have deliberately or passively threatened the lives of Native Americans, African Americans, and Latinos through social, economic, and political policies in the form of environmental racism—the inequitable exposure of people of color to air, water, and noise pollution on a scale sufficient to trigger birth defects, miscarriages, stillbirths, cancer, and stress-related illnesses documented since the 1980s. Environmental justice seeks to eliminate such racism by demanding equitable treatment for people of color and the poor through government policy, legislation, regulation, and law enforcement. Environmental justice activists have employed many of the same strategies as civil rights activists to counter environmental racism, including lobbying, legislation, law enforcement, and protest.

Such organized resistance is not new to African Americans. For example, in the 1917 New York City Silent Protest Parade approximately ten thousand African Americans marched peacefully with banners against racism by whites. Founded upon this early twentieth-century history of resistance, a national social and political movement initiated by African Americans and their supporters later crisscrossed the United States. African Americans struggled through boycotts, marches, freedom rides, sit-ins, and protests. People throughout the world witnessed the events of the 1950s and 1960s, hearing, watching, and reading the news media of radio, television, and newspaper, which shamed the U.S. government and white Southern citizenry. As a result of the scrutiny and, more important, the dedication of civil rights leaders and volunteers, the activism culminated with the Civil Rights Act of 1964, which legally banned discrimination in public places, including restaurants and transportation systems, and the Voting Rights Act of 1965, which authorized federal employees to register African Americans to vote while suspending discriminatory literacy tests and poll taxes that once barred African Americans from doing so.

Against this backdrop, African American ministers and civil rights activists were catalysts leading peaceful demonstrations. Dwight N. Hopkins says that Christian leaders of the civil rights era "religiously told white officials to stick to Christian love and nonviolence . . . [and] preached funerals for nonviolent civil rights workers. And they experienced the pain of having their churches dynamited in the early morning hours."[2] As president of the Southern Christian Leadership Conference (SCLC), a civil rights protest organization, King helped to define civil rights activism in his 1963 "Letter from a Birmingham Jail" addressed to his fellow clergy and concerning injustice:

> Just as the prophets of the eighth century B.C. left their villages and carried their 'thus saith the Lord' far beyond the boundaries of their home towns, and just as the Apostle Paul left his village of Tarsus and carried the gospel of Jesus Christ to the far corners of the Greco-Roman world, so am I compelled to carry the gospel of freedom beyond my own home town.

Much of this history serves as context to the issue of environmental racism by whites and the history of environmental justice by the African American church and Christian organizations. Environ-

mental justice activists in the African American church—part of the
long history of the civil rights movement in the African American
community—struggled to reverse twentieth-century environmental
racism. Robert Bullard, author of *Unequal Protection: Environmental
Justice and Communities of Color* (1994), refers briefly to King's role
in the 1968 Memphis, Tennessee, Sanitation Worker's Strike, the
precursor to late twentieth- and twenty-first-century environmental
justice activism.[3] The strike deserves a closer look. On February 12,
1968, the Memphis sanitation workers went on strike to improve
wages, hours, and vacations, with an unhealthy work environment as
a subtext. Sanitation workers handling the city's trash were exposed
to hospital waste and rotting food, which drew rodents, roaches,
and birds, creating a petri-dish environment that led to rashes and
disease. In the words of Leroy Bonner, a sanitation worker:

> [One time there were] two maggots right around my navel. I
> took a bath and they stretched out and they fell off in the tub.
> And my wife said, "Lord have mercy, Leroy, wait a minute and
> let me run that water out" . . . She ran it out and she came in
> and washed my head and everything, and [she] was pulling
> them out of my head. You see, that was summertime. I said,
> "Well, I can't help it . . . We got to try to make it."[4]

Bonner's exposure to rotting trash and maggots indicated how
race and poverty defined the status and treatment of African Americans in the 1960s. As a poor African American man who had limited
choices for employment, his work environment was a hostile place.

African American ministers, local leaders, and church members
joined sanitation workers like Bonner to organize a citywide strike
and boycott on February 24. A day later, the ministers requested
that their congregations support the sanitation boycott and march

on behalf of the workers. Throughout March, Henry Loeb, the mayor of Memphis, met with the ministers, who continued to lead marches while their congregations raised money by holding a gospel music marathon.[5] The strike grew nationally when King led a rally on March 18. Later, on April 3, King spoke at the Mason Temple in Memphis, Tennessee, supporting the sanitation workers in his famous speech "I've Been to the Mountaintop":

> There are thirteen hundred of God's children here suffer-
> ing, sometimes going hungry, going through dark and dreary
> nights wondering how this thing is going to come out. . . . It's
> all right to talk about streets flowing with milk and honey,
> but God has commanded us to be concerned about the slums
> down here and his children who can't eat three square meals a
> day. It's all right to talk about the new Jerusalem, but one day
> God's preacher must talk about the new New York, the new
> Atlanta, the new Philadelphia, the new Los Angeles, the new
> Memphis, Tennessee.[6]

King's vision for improving the living conditions of poor African Americans was inherently environmental. He addressed the complexities of wages, safety, and health, giving the plight of sanitation workers context, mindful of the environmental problems in the inner city during the civil rights era. King's speech also evoked something broader—"a moral geography of social and political progress"—and constituted an implicit environmental manifesto decrying and aiming to dismantle everything from slavery to segregation set against the stage of nature.

After the 1960s, Benjamin F. Chavis Jr., at one time a reverend and the president of the National Association for the Advancement of Colored People (NAACP), criticized environmental justice as a national movement and advocated specifically for African

Americans. At the 1993 National Black Church Environmental and Economic Justice Summit, he referred implicitly to whites and explicitly to African Americans as being culpable concerning the environment:

> The fact that we [African Americans] are disproportionately dumped on is just consistent with being in America . . . And the demand that God puts on us is that we will face up to the contemporary responsibility that God has given us to not let God's creation be destroyed by sin . . . Environmental injustice is sin before God."[7]

Chavis's historical and activist role in Warren County, North Carolina, was part of the modern catalyst for the national environmental justice movement. In 1978 liquid tank drivers hired by the Ward Transformer Company secretly poured toxic man-made PCBs, or polychlorinated biphenyls, along roads across thirteen North Carolina counties. In an attempt to dispose of the tainted soil, the state of North Carolina constructed a landfill in Warren County, which was predominantly African American.[8] In 1984, African American leaders like Chavis joined Warren County citizens to demonstrate against the government's attempt to collect and then dump the soil in the county backyard. Other church leaders, including Reverend Joseph Lowery of the Southern Christian Leadership Conference, and Walter Fauntroy, a Progressive National Baptist minister, united with locals to peacefully protest the dumping. They were concerned about the correlation of PCBs with various illnesses, including skin disorders, reproductive problems, liver disease, and cancer. African American women mixed prayer and supplication with activism in a rural Baptist church. Though these women, along with other protestors, failed when they were arrested, they ignited national environmental justice activism.

The Commission for Racial Justice of the United Church of Christ sought social justice for African Americans, later expanding to include other people of color, by picketing with the Student Nonviolent Coordinating Committee during civil rights protests and participating in the 1972 National Black Political Convention in Gary, Indiana.[9] The Commission continued its commitment to environmental justice, evident in the landmark study *Toxic Wastes and Race in the United States: A National Report on the Racial and Socio-Economic Characteristics of Communities with Hazardous Waste Sites* (1987). Chavis explained the United Church of Christ's decision to complement its activism with a publication for environmental justice advocacy:

> We believe that the time has come for all church and civil rights organizations to take the issues seriously. We realized that the involvement in this type of research is a departure from our traditional protest methodology. However, if we are to advance our struggle in the future, it will depend largely on the availability of timely and reliable information.[10]

This report remains a critical source for studying and further developing the environmental justice movement. Later, in 1994, the commission also responded when Shintech planned, but eventually failed, to construct a polyvinyl chloride manufacturing plant in Convent, Louisiana.

Locally, grassroots organizations fought environmental racism through activism. Since 1977, the Reichhold Chemical Company located in Columbia, Mississippi, had been accused of exposing two hundred cattle to dioxins and exploding Agent Orange, a defoliant herbicide and dioxin. In addition, the company allegedly poured chemicals downstream into Jingling Creek, past a recreational facility and high school frequented by African Americans. Four floods also exposed toxins that Reichold had buried off-site, at what is now a Superfund site. In 1992, Jesus People Against Pollution (JPAP) established a grassroots environmental justice organization, responding to years of toxic dumping by Reichold.[11] JPAP exposed Reichold's disregard for the community and the resulting health problems and increased mortality among African Americans.

During the 1990s, Helping Other People Emerge (HOPE), an organization established by Reverend Buck Jones in East St. Louis, drew upon environmental activism and Christian faith. Locals approached HOPE because they had been shaken out of bed at 3:00 A.M., their windows and dishes broken and the foundations of their homes cracked by a shredding company that was putting cars, including contaminated vehicles with gasoline tanks, into the shredder, which caused explosions. According to Jones, "We marched, we prayed, we threatened to file a lawsuit, we blocked the entranceway to the plant, and we won. They [the shredder company] hired residents to check and inspect the cars; in addition, they also gave a cash settlement." He organized projects reducing lead poisoning among children, the cleaning up of Dead Creek, and a rally against Onyx Environmental Services, which planned to incinerate neutralized nerve gas for the United States Army at the expense of local African Americans. Before Jones's death, he organized toxic tours of East St. Louis, exposing toxic hotspots and the role of the government and corporations in environmental racism in the city.[12]

Jones based his final initiatives on the efforts of the National Council of Churches (NCC), which consolidated grassroots action into a national effort in December 1993. Leaders of the major African American churches—including the African Methodist Episcopal; African Methodist Episcopal Zion; National Baptist Convention, USA; National Baptist Convention of America; Progressive National Baptist Convention; and the Church of God in Christ—met for two days at the National Black Church Environmental and Economic Justice Summit in Washington, D.C.[13] The attendees emphasized quality of life and health in the African American community, focusing on pollution and dumping rather than the mainstream interests of eliminating global ozone depletion and protecting endangered species.[14] Reverend W. Franklyn Richardson, the general secretary of the National Baptist Convention, USA, presented Vice President Al Gore Jr. with six demands in the NCC report, including a recommendation for a presidential executive order on environmental justice and regulation of corporations. Two demands focused on the African American church: identifying a church representative for the Sustainable Communities Task Force of the President's Council on Sustainable Development and involving local churches in key environmental decisions by the government. These suggestions indicated ways that African Americans could influence government environmental policy.

On March 13 and 14, 1998, approximately twelve African American church leaders toured toxic sites in Louisiana communities, including Convent, Oakville, New Sarpy, and Norco, a tangible outcome of the NCC Summit. The NCC Eco-Justice Working Group, the Black Church Liaison Committee, and the United States Conference of the World Council of Churches sponsored the tours. The leaders traveled around communities polluted by polyvinyl chloride (PVC), a toxic dump, and "fumes, explosions, and fires" from twenty-seven oil refineries. They scheduled a meeting with Gore, which was ultimately canceled, to plead the case of the Louisiana communities.[15]

With the arrival of Hurricane Katrina in August 2005, people in Louisiana, including New Orleans, faced other forms of environmental devastation. Prior to the hurricane the city was a beautiful place filled with parties and festivals as the temperatures shifted from hot to warm to cool. But beneath the festive surface were very poor people, African Americans, who represented a majority of the

New Orleans population. Many lived in the lowest-lying areas of the city in run-down homes unfit for any human.

When the hurricane hit, African Americans were trapped all across New Orleans, and many of them died. Unlike whites and the more affluent, many poor African American, elderly, and physically and mentally ill residents did not have access to transportation to escape the city, which left them more vulnerable to the environmental devastation of Katrina. Some said the hurricane was God's way of punishing a sinful people in a sinful city. In reality, television sets streamed terrifying images of African Americans battling nature, reflections of the broader strokes of institutional and structural racism that encompass environmental racism.

The plight of African Americans exposed to disease by the putrid waters in New Orleans echoes the experience of Africans who died of disease and starvation after they were captured by whites in Africa and transported to the Americas in the dark holds of ships during the Middle Passage. Similarly, African Americans wading through the post-Katrina muck mirrored the African Americans who survived the 1927 Mississippi flood. As was true during slavery, towns and cities along the Mississippi were rebuilt on the backs of African Americans, as they were forced and coerced into repairing the levees after the flood. In the twenty-first century, Central American immigrants from places like Mexico and Guatemala did the backbreaking work after Katrina.

Since enslavement ended, the vision for racial equality has been deferred in the United States. In 1865 Alexander Crummell, an African American theologian, said, "The trials and suffering of this race have been great for centuries. They have not yet ceased. They are not likely to cease for a long time. It may take two to three generations for the race to get a firm and assured status in the land."[16] Crummell would be alarmed at the tenuous standing of third-generation

African Americans undermined by environmental racism into the twenty-first century. In response to being inequitably exposed to toxic chemicals, waste, and environmental devastation caused by nature, however, African Americans have continued their legacy of resistance, combining grassroots activism, spirituality, and organization to craft a "spearhead for reform" that African Americans who continue to be embattled by environmental racism can carry into the future.

Conclusion

HERITAGE AND THE FUTURE

Carmen's ancestor Minkah would have appreciated the scene before her. Carmen is standing in one of the White House gardens, the vegetable garden, along with her classmates, her teacher, the Secret Service, and the First Lady of the United States. Everyone is nervous about the Secret Service but also wondering if the president will show up. The children crowd around the First Lady, and she tells them that the garden is organic, which is healthier for everyone. No pesticides. No chemical fertilizers. Carmen bends down and picks up a handful of earth, thinking of stories of Minkah. Her mother says people in the family said Minkah was a priest who guarded an earth shrine. The stories were passed down because many family members stayed in Alabama, where he had lived. Carmen looks up; the First Lady stands blocking the sunlight. They smile at each other and nod. Something has passed between them. Maybe it is the memories of Africans, including priests and farmers, whom African Americans emulate today, returning to the land.

When First Lady Michelle Obama planted a vegetable garden on the grounds of the White House, her goal was to promote healthy eating among schoolchildren. From the first shovel of soil to the first harvest of ripe vegetables by a group of Washington, D.C. fifth graders, the White House garden project has served as an educational tool for children of different ethnicities, including African Americans, who pick the vegetables from the vine and cook the produce themselves.

Many people do not know the source of the water in their glasses, the chicken on their plates, or the potatoes in their ovens. African Americans are no exception. We need to reconnect to the land because knowledge of the environment and access to resources, from the roots in the ground to the broader political landscape, can determine who will enjoy high-quality lives.

President Obama has long had a progressive environmental agenda. He ran on a platform focusing on health care, energy, education, and the economy. Concerning energy, he plans to generate 25 percent of the United States' energy from clean, renewable energy sources—solar, wind, biofuels, and geothermal power—rather than petroleum by the year 2025.[1] The president and First Lady's work continues on the international stage. At the December 2009 Copenhagen climate summit, President Obama gave a speech acknowledging to the world that the United States was contributing to the environmental problems that plague the planet. The president said, "We must choose action over inaction, the future over the past—with courage and faith, let us meet our responsibility to our people, and to the future of our planet."[2]

This book began in Africa with the enslaved crossing the Atlantic into the Americas. It continued in time from enslavement to freedom to the African diaspora and ends with children in the garden of the nation's first African American president and First Lady. We can reclaim our environmental heritage, but no one needs to step into a void. Locally, nationally, and internationally, blacks can follow the inspirational examples of our forefathers and -mothers' unique relationship with the land, the civil rights generation's strategies for change, and contemporaries such as the Obamas' sense of environmental stewardship. We have templates for environmental change and reengagement. We can—no, *we must*—answer the call.

Acknowledgments

I thank my parents and grandparents, my environmental muses, who introduced me to nature, so different from the concrete and asphalt of Queens, New York. In addition, my parents and brother were and continue to be my emotional support. Other family members—Sandra, Ishmael, Melissa, and Christina Morgan; Vernice and Aston Glaves; and Rupert and Marsyl DePass—gave me immeasurable moral support.

At Lawrence Hill Books, I would like to thank editors Susan Betz and Lisa Reardon, who provided invaluable feedback.

Resources

Booker T. Washington National Monument

12130 Booker T. Washington Highway

Hardy, Virginia 24101

(540) 721-2094

www.nps.gov/bowa/index.htm

This 207-acre property reconstructs a middle-class tobacco farm, representative of the conditions in which Booker T. Washington spent his enslaved childhood. This area was the birthplace and early childhood home of the famous African American leader and educator. Through the presentation of historic buildings, gardens, crafts, and animals, the monument provides background about Washington's life and achievements, as well as about 1850s slavery and farming.

George Washington Carver National Monument

5646 Carver Road

Diamond, Missouri 64840

(417) 325-4151

www.nps.gov/gwca/index.htm

This 210-acre property preserves the site of the boyhood home of George Washington Carver. The property features the Carver Nature Trail, Carver Science Classroom, 1881 Moses Carver House, the Carver Museum, and more.

The Harriet Tubman Home
180 South Street

Auburn, New York 13201

(315) 252-2081

www.nyhistory.com/harriettubman

For a better understanding of Harriet Tubman's environmental experiences, visit the Harriet Tubman Home, operated by the AME Zion Church. Motherland Connextions (www.motherlandconnextions.com/tours.html) offers tours of the Underground Railroad, highlighting the Niagara Falls region and Tubman's numerous treks from the South to the North.

Mystic Seaport—The Museum of America and the Sea
75 Greenmanville Avenue

Mystic, Connecticut 06355

(860) 572-5315 or (888) 973-2767

www.mysticseaport.org

This museum has several resources to learn more about blacks in maritime America, including public exhibitions and archives. Visit a nineteenth-century village and learn about shipbuilding from the period. See the many exhibitions, including "Tugs," all about tugboats. The schooner *Amistad* (www.amistadamerica.org) is a sailing museum that is supported in part by the Mystic Seaport museum.

National Park Service

www.nps.gov/index.htm

Get back to nature by visiting one of the many national parks across the United States. Go to the Biscayne National Park in Florida to see the wonders of coral reefs. Travel to the West to experience waterfalls, valleys, and the sequoias in California. Take a special trip to the African Burial Ground National Monument, a memorial to blacks who were enslaved and buried in Lower Manhattan.

ORGANIZATIONS

The Black Farmers and Agriculturalists Association (BFAA)

P.O. Box 61

Tillery, North Carolina 27887

(252) 826-2800

www.bfaa-us.org/index.html

The Black Farmers and Agriculturalists Association (BFAA) is a grassroots volunteer organization created in 1997 to address the sharp decline in the number of African American farmers and landowners and to advocate for them. Its membership includes farmers and agriculturalists, concerned citizens, activists, and academics.

Earthwise Productions, Inc.

450 Piedmont Avenue, Suite #1512

Atlanta, Georgia 30308

(404) 875-1375

http://earthwiseproductionsinc.com

The purpose of this organization is to spread information to diverse groups of people who generally do not frequent national parks. Earthwise provides tours for those who are unfamiliar with the parks and publishes a periodical called *Pickup and GO!* that reaches out to an urban audience to generate more interests in the parks.

Green for All

1611 Telegraph Avenue, Suite 600

Oakland, California 94612

(510) 663-6500

www.greenforall.org

Green for All is a national nonprofit organization working to improve the lives of all Americans, particularly the most vulnerable, through a clean-energy economy. The group works in collaboration with the business, government, labor, and grassroots communities to develop and implement programs that create jobs and opportunities in green industry.

Keeping It Wild

817 West Peachtree Street, NW, Suite 200

Atlanta, Georgia 30308

(678) 904-2200

www.keepingitwild.org

Launched in 1985 by community members in the Atlanta metro area, Keeping It Wild advocates for people of color and the environment in Georgia. The group hosts a wide range of outdoor outings and educational seminars and emphasizes environmental sustainability in the wild in Georgia and throughout the Southeast.

Southeastern African-American Farmers Organic Network (SAAFON)

P.O. Box 456

Savannah, Georgia 31402

(912) 495-0591

www.saafon.org

SAAFON is a network of small and limited-resource farmers who are either certified organic or growing organically. The site includes information about SAAFON's goals, farmers, special projects, farmers markets, youth camps, and more.

Sustainable South Bronx (SSBx)
890 Garrison Avenue, 4th Floor
Bronx, New York 10474
(646) 400-5430
www.ssbx.org
This nonprofit organization blends the economic and environmental goals of building sustainable urban communities in the Bronx. SSBx emphasizes issues central to quality of life, including transportation and waste management.

WEB SITES

Breaking the Color Barrier in the Great American Outdoors
www.breakingthecolorbarrier.com
This Web site, dedicated to the 2009 conference of the same name, includes information on the various speakers and links to many media stories about people of color and nature.

The Library of Congress
http://memory.loc.gov/
Learn more about African Americans and the environment by accessing the "Liberation Strategies" collection, which contains primary sources, available online at the Library of Congress (http://memory.loc.gov/ammem/aaohtml/aopart1.html#01b). For a closer inspection of David Walker's *Appeal*, a pamphlet with environmental references by an African American man decrying enslavement during the period of the American Revolution, visit the LOC Reading Room (www.loc.gov/rr/rarebook/).

The National Parks: America's Best Idea

People: Shelton Johnson

www.pbs.org/nationalparks/people/nps/johnson/

http://shadowsoldier.wilderness.net

Shelton Johnson has worked for the National Park Service since 1987 and is currently one of the few African American park rangers at Yosemite Park. Information about his life, photos, and a link to his novel can be found on this PBS site for Ken Burns's documentary *The National Parks: America's Best Idea* and on Johnson's Web site, http://shadowsoldier.wilderness.net.

Outdoor Afro

http://outdoorafro.com/

Headlined "Where Black People and Nature Meet," Rue Mapp's Web site is devoted to African Americans interested in getting closer to nature through recreation like skiing and hiking. She includes a blog, Facebook link, photos, and more.

"Places for the Spirit: Traditional African American Gardens of the South"

www.vaughnsills.com/gardens/index.htm

This online portfolio of photographer Vaughn Sills features images of traditional African American gardens and includes an artist statement describing the series.

Notes

INTRODUCTION: PEOPLE AND CURRENTS

Epigraph. Thomas Monroe Campbell, *The Movable School Goes to the Negro Farmer* (Tuskegee, AL: Tuskegee Institute Press, 1936), 48.

1. Wendell Berry, *Sex, Economy, Freedom, and Community: Eight Essays* (New York: Pantheon Books, 1993), 27.

2. George Washington Carver, "Being Kind to the Soil," *The Negro Farmer* (January 31, 1941); Theodore Rosengarten, comp. *All God's Dangers: The Life of Nate Shaw* (New York: Vintage Books, 1989), 77. Ned Cobb's pseudonym in the narrative is Nate Shaw.

3. Campbell, 149.

4. Mart Stewart, "Slavery and the Origins of African American Environmentalism," in *"To Love the Wind and the Rain": African Americans and the Environment*, ed. Dianne D. Glave and Mark Stoll (Pittsburgh: University of Pittsburgh Press, 2006), 19; Mark Stoll, "Religion and African American Activism," in *"To Love the Wind and the Rain": African Americans and the Environment*, ed. Dianne D. Glave and Mark Stoll (Pittsburgh: University of Pittsburgh Press, 2006), 160; and Dianne Glave, "What's Next for African American Environmental History?"

Parts 1 and 2. *ASEH News* vol. 17, nos. 1 and 2 (Spring and Summer 2006): 9–12.

1   THE ATLANTIC OCEAN: CURRENTS OF LIFE AND DEATH

1. W. Jeffrey Bolster, *Black Jacks: African American Seamen in the Age of Sail* (Cambridge, MA: Harvard University Press, 1997), 2.

2. Ivan Van Sertima, *They Came Before Columbus: The African Presence in Ancient Africa* (New York: Random House, 2003), 41–42.

3. Ibid., 42.

4. Ibid., 42.

5. Thomas Bluett, *Some Memoirs of the Life of Job, the Son of Solomon the High Priest of Boonda in Africa; Who was a Slave about Two Years in Maryland* (London, Printed for Richard Ford, 1734), Eighteenth Century Collections Online, Emory University, Robert W. Woodruff Library, http://galenet.galegroup.com.proxy.library.emory.edu/, 25.

6. Ibid., 26.

7. Olaudah Equiano, *Equiano's Travels: His Autobiography the Interesting Narrative of the Life of Olaudah Equiano or Gustavus Vassa the African* (London: Heinemann, 1980), 28–29.

8. Ibid., 30.

9. Ibid., 107.

10. Ibid., 44.

11. Nancy Prince, *A Black Woman's Odyssey Through Russia and Jamaica: The Narrative of Nancy Prince* (New York: Marcus Weiner Publishing, 1990), 76–77.

12. Harry Dean, *The Pedro Gorino: The Adventures of a Negro Sea-Captain in Africa on the Seven Seas in His Attempts to Found an Ethiopian Empire, An Autobiographical Narrative* (Boston: Houghton Mifflin Co., 1929), 15–16, 26.

13. Frederick Douglass, *Narrative of the Life of Frederick Douglass, An American Slave* (New York: Library of America, 1994), 73; Harriet Jacobs, *Incidents in the Life of a Slave Girl* (New York: Modern Library, 2000), 68.

14. Charles Johnson, *Middle Passage* (New York: Scribner, 1998), 4.

15. Bolster, 4.

16. Interview, Rue Mapp, January 10, 2010. See also outdoorafro.com, Mapp's Web site.

2 TOPOGRAPHY: NAVIGATING THE SOUTHERN LANDSCAPE

1. Sam Hilliard, *Atlas of Antebellum Southern Agriculture* (Baton Rouge: Louisiana State University Press, 1984), 7–10; Rupert Vance, *Human Geography of the South: A Study in Regional Resources and Human Adequacy* (1932; repr., New York: Russell and Russell, 1968), 27.

2. Mart Stewart, "Slavery and the Origins of African American Environmentalism," in *"To Love the Wind and the Rain": African Americans and the Environment*, ed. Dianne D. Glave and Mark Stoll (Pittsburgh: University of Pittsburgh Press, 2006), 16; Frederick Douglass, *Autobiographies: Narrative of the Life of Frederick Douglass, an American Slave; My Bondage and My Freedom; Life and Times of Frederick Douglass* (New York: Library of America, 1994), 73–74.

3. W. E. B. DuBois, *The Quest of the Silver Fleece* (New York: Arno Press, 1969), 150–51.

4. A. Cash Koeniger, "Climate and Southern Distinctiveness," *Journal of Southern History* 54, no. 1 (February 1988): 26; Merrick Posnansky, "Anatomy of a Continent," in *The Africans: A Reader*, ed. Ali A. Mazrui and Toby Kleban Levine (New York: Praeger, 1986), 47; Mart Stewart, "'Let Us Begin with the Weather?': Climate, Race, and Cultural Distinctiveness in the American South," in *Nature and Society in*

Historical Context, ed. Mikuláš Teich, Roy Porter, and Bo Gustafsson (Cambridge: Cambridge University Press, 1997), 243.

5. Charles L. Perdue Jr., Thomas E. Barden, and Robert K. Phillips, eds., *Weevils in the Wheat: Interviews with Virginia Ex-Slaves* (Charlottesville: University Press of Virginia, 1976), 32.

6. Theodore Rosengarten, comp., *All God's Dangers: The Life of Nate Shaw.* (1974; repr., New York: Vintage Books, 1989), 181, 183.

7. Ibid., 15–17.

8. Ibid., 24–25.

9. William Cronon, *Changes in the Land: Indians, Colonists, and the Ecology of New England* (New York: Hill and Wang, 1983), ix; Donald Worster, "Transformation of the Earth: Toward an Agroecological Perspective in History," *Journal of American History* 76 (March 1990): 1093–94.

10. DuBois, 54 and 78.

11. Booker T. Washington, *The Booker T. Washington Papers*, vol. 1, 261, 322, Washington, Booker T, "Atlanta Compromise," http://history matters.gmu.edu/d/39/, reprinted from *The Booker T. Washington Papers*, vol. 3, ed. Louis R. Harlan (Champaign: University of Illinois Press, 1974), 583–87.

12. Victor Ernest Shelford, *The Ecology of North America* (1963; repr., Urbana: University of Illinois Press, 1978), 39, 40, 57, 78, 89; Vance, 86.

13. "Clara Cotton McCoy," *Born in Slavery: Slave Narratives from the Federal Writers' Project, 1936–1938, North Carolina Narratives*, vol. 11, pt. 2, American Memory, Library of Congress, National Digital Library Program, http://memory.loc.gov, 68; Washington, *The Booker T. Washington Papers*, vol. 1, 217; Cassandra Johnson and Josh McDaniel, "Turpentine Negro," in *"To Love the Wind and the Rain": African Americans and Environmental History*, ed. Dianne D. Glave and Mark Stoll (Pittsburgh: University of Pittsburgh Press, 2006), 51–6.

3   RELIGION: SHOUTING IN THE WOODS

1. Eric C. Lincoln and Lawrence H. Mamiya, "The Religious Dimension: 'The Black Sacred Cosmos,'" in *Down by the Riverside: Readings in African American Religion*, ed. Larry G. Murphy (New York: New York University Press, 2000), 32; Maulana Karenga, "Black Religion: The African Model," in *Down by the Riverside: Readings in African American Religion*, ed. Larry G. Murphy (New York: New York University Press, 2000), 42–44; Dominique Zahan, "Some Reflections of African Spirituality," in *African Spirituality: Forms, Meanings, and Expressions*, ed. Jacob K. Olupona (New York: Crossroads Publishing, 2000), 5, 16–17, 20–21, 23, 27; Melville Herskovits, *Dahomey: An Ancient West African Kingdom* vol. 2. (Evanston: Northwestern University Press, 1938), 171; Wyatt MacGaffey, "Complexity, Astonishment, and Power: The Visual Vocabulary of Kongo Minkisi," *Journal of Southern African Studies* 14, no. 2 (1988): 189–203.

2.   Zora Neale Hurston, *The Sanctified Church* (Berkeley: Turtle Island, 1983), 91.

3. Harriet Jacobs, *Incidents in the Life of a Slave Girl* (New York: W. W. Norton, 2001), 80, 92–93; Ywone D. Edwards, "'Trash' Revisited: A Comparative Approach to Historical Descriptions and Archeological Analysis of Slave Houses and Yards," in *Keep Your Head to the Sky: Interpreting African American Home Ground*, ed. Grey Gundaker (Charlottesville: University Press of Virginia, 1998), 266; Robert Farris Thompson, *Flash of the Spirit: Africa and Afro-American Art and Philosophy* (New York: Random House, 1983), 8–9.

4. James L. Wilson, *Clementine Hunter: American Folk Artist* (Gretna, LA: Pelican Publishing, 1988), 9, 30; Shelby R. Gilley, *Painting by Heart: The Life and Art of Clementine Hunter, Louisiana Folk Artist* (Baton Rouge: St. Emma Press, 2000), 60.

5. DuBois, 3; Wilson, 30, 68; Mark 1:1–5 (King James Version).

6. Wilmore, 99–124.

7. Genesis 2:7 (King James Version); Charles L. Perdue, Thomas A. Barden, and Robert K. Phillips, eds., *Weevils in the Wheat: Interviews with Virginia Ex-Slaves* (Charlottesville: University Press of Virginia, 1976), 224; Riggins R. Earl, Jr., *Dark Symbols, Obscure Signs: God, Self, and Community in the Slave Mind* (Maryknoll, NY: Orbis Books, 1993), 47–49.

8. Kelly Brown Douglas, *The Black Christ* (Maryknoll, NY: Orbis Books, 1993), 24; Edwin S. Redkey, ed., *Respect Black: The Writings and Speeches of Henry McNeal Turner* (New York: Arno Press, 1971), 176–77; Elly M. Wynia, *The Church of God and Saints of Christ: The Rise of Black Jews.* (New York: Garland Books, 1994), 13–15.

9. Clifton H. Johnson, *God Struck Me Dead: Religious Conversion Experiences and Autobiographies of Ex-Slaves* (Philadelphia: Pilgrim Press, 1969). For the conversion experiences of white Protestants in nature, which were described as more circumspect and formal than those of African Americans, see Jeannine Hensley, ed. *The Works of Ann Bradstreet* (1678; repr., Cambridge, MA: Belknap Press of Harvard University Press, 1967) and Jonathan Edwards, *The Works of Jonathan Edwards* (1842; repr., Peabody: Hendrickson Publishers, 1998).

10. Perdue, 320. Conversion according to the Bible is outlined in Romans 6:1–23 (King James Version).

11. Johnson, 3.

12. Johnson, 15; Matthew 28:19–20 (King James Version).

13. Carter G. Woodson, *The African Background Outlined* (1936; repr., New York: Negro Universities Press, 1968), 358.

14. "Molly Jordan: Mulatto Farm Woman," November 1, 1938, Federal Writer's Project Papers, Folder 442, Box 3709, Southern Historical Collection, Library of the University of North Carolina of Chapel Hill, 5700.

15. Toni Morrison, *Beloved* (New York: Plume Books USA, 1987), 87–88.

4 RESISTANCE: REBELLION, SUSTENANCE, AND ESCAPE IN THE WILDERNESS

1. David Walker, *Appeal: To the Colored Citizens of the World, but in Particular, and Very Expressly, to those of the United States of America* (New York: Hill and Wang, 1965), 3–4.

2. Frederick Douglass, "What to the Slave is the 4th of July?" The Freeman Institute, http://www.freemaninstitute.com/douglass.htm.

3. Boyrereau Brinch, *The Blind African Slave, or Memoirs of Boyrereau Brinch, Nick-named Jeffrey Brace. Containing an Account of the Kingdom of Bow-Woo, in the Interior of Africa; with the Climate and Natural Productions, Laws, and Customs Peculiar to That Place. With an Account of His Captivity, Sufferings, Sales, Travels, Emancipation, Conversion to the Christian Religion, Knowledge of the Scriptures, &c. Interspersed with Strictures on Slavery, Speculative Observations on the Qualities of Human Nature, with Quotation from Scripture, Documenting the South* (St. Albans, VT: Printed by Harry Whitney, 1810), http://docsouth.unc.edu/neh/brinch/brinch.html, 71.

4. Ibid., 91, 93.

5. Howard Jones, *Mutiny on the Amistad: The Saga of a Slave Revolt and Its Impact on American Abolition, Law, and Diplomacy* (New York: Oxford University Press, 1987), 22–24, 26–28.

6. Eugene D. Genovese, *The Political Economy of Slavery: Studies in the Economy and Society of the Slave South* (Middleton, CT: Wesleyan University Press, 1989), 55, 111, 113.

7. Nicolas W. Proctor, *Bathed in Blood: Hunting and Mastery in the Old South* (Charlottesville: University Press of Virginia, 2002), 144, 152–54; Scott Giltner, "Slave Hunting and Fishing in the Antebellum South," in *"To Love the Wind and the Rain": African Americans and the Environment*, ed. Dianne D. Glave and Mark Stoll (Pittsburgh: University of Pittsburgh Press, 2006), 21–36.

8. Thomas Wentworth Higginson, *Black Rebellion: A Selection from Travellers and Outlaws* (New York: Arno Press, 1969), 121, 123; Kenneth M. Bilby, *True-Born Maroons* (Gainesville: University Press of Florida, 2005), 99.

9. Bilby, 129, 131–32, 136, 176–79, 150–52; Nancy Prince, *A Black Woman's Odyssey Through Russia and Jamaica: The Narrative of Nancy Prince* (New York: Marcus Weiner Publishing, 1990), 62.

10. Nat Turner, "The Confession, Trial and Execution of Nat Turner," in *The Nat Turner Slave Insurrection* by F. Roy Johnson (Murfreesboro, N.C.: Johnson Publishing Co., 1966), 230, 232–34, 243.

11. Catherine Clinton, *Harriet Tubman: The Road to Freedom* (New York: Little Brown and Company, 2004), 34, 84, 87.

12. "Dog Fighting: An Historical Note," The Humane Society, http://www.peoriahs.org/dogfighthistory.htm; Proctor, 164.

5 PRESERVATION: BLENDING THE PRACTICAL AND THE PURIST

1. Mary L. Oberlin, "Learn to Live on a Farm," *The Negro Farmer and Messenger,* April 8, 1916.

2. Ralph Lutts, *The Nature Fakers: Wildlife, Science, and Sentiment* (Golden, CO: Fulcrum, 1990), 1–12; John Muir, *John Muir: Writings*, ed. William Cronon (New York: Library of America, 1997); Carolyn Merchant, "The Women of the Progressive Conservation Crusade: 1900–1915," in *Environmental History: Critical Issues in Comparative Perspective*, ed. Kendall Bailes (Lanham, MD: University Press of America, 1985), 159–60.

3. "Priori Travel Guides," http://www.btinternet.com/~stuart.melvin/html/matopos.html; Terence Ranger, *Voices from the Rock: Nature, Culture, and History in the Matopos Hills of Zimbabwe* (Bloomington: Indiana University Press, 1999), 16.

4. W. E. B. DuBois, *The Quest of the Silver Fleece* (New York: Arno Press, 1969); Zora Neale Hurston, *Zora Neale Hurston: Novels and Stories* (New York: Library of America, 1995), 173–333; Jean Toomer, *Cane* (New York: Norton, 1988), 123–28.

5. Robert B. Outland III, *Tapping the Pines: The Naval Stores Industry in the American South* (Baton Rouge: Louisiana State University Press, 2004), 102–04.

6. Mart A. Stewart, *"What Nature Suffers to Groe": Life, Labor, and Landscape on the Georgia Coast, 1680–1920* (Athens: University of Georgia Press, 2002), 210; James E. Fickle, *Timber: A Photographic History of Mississippi Forestry* (Jackson: Mississippi Forestry Foundation and the University Press of Mississippi, 2004), 83–86; "Negro Worker at a Small Sawmill Works in Southern Greene County, Georgia," LC-USF33-020953-M3, Library of Congress Prints and Photographs Division, http://loc.gov; "Untitled," LC-USF33-020953-M4, Library of Congress Prints and Photographs Division, http://loc.gov [accessed May 20, 2005].

7. Toomer, 3–4.

8. Ibid., 3–4, 15.

9. John Biggers, *My America, the 1940s and 1950s: Paintings, Sculpture, and Drawings* (New Orleans: Michael Rosenfeld Gallery, 2005), 46, 55–62.

6 CONSERVATION: AN AFRICAN LEGACY OF WORKING THE LAND

1. Lewis W. Jones, "South Negro Farm Agent," *Journal of Negro Education* 38 (Winter 1953): 43.

2. Mart A. Stewart, *"What Nature Suffers to Groe": Life, Labor, and Landscape on the Georgia Coast, 1680–1920* (Athens: University of Georgia Press, 2002), 135.

3. Carolyn Merchant, ed., *Major Problems in American Environmental History* (Lexington, MA: D.C. Heath, 1993), vii.

4. Joseph M. Petulla, *American Environmental History: The Exploitation and Conservation of Natural Resources* (San Francisco: Boyd and Fraser Publishing, 1977), 267; Samuel P. Hays, *Conservation and the Gospel of Efficiency: The Progressive Conservation Movement, 1890–1920* (Cambridge, MA: Harvard University Press, 1959), 122.

5. Terracing creates horizontal ridges carved into a hillside to increase cultivatable land, conserve moisture, and minimize wind and water erosion. Robert Soper, *Nyanga: Ancient Fields Settlements, and Agricultural History in Zimbabwe* (London: British Institute of Eastern Africa, 2002), 2, 22, 29; Keith Hart, *The Political Economy of West African Agriculture* (Cambridge: Cambridge University Press, 1982), 56.

6. Adrian Adams and Jaabe So, *A Claim to Land by the River* (New York: Oxford University Press, 1996), 36–37.

7. Judith A. Carney, *Black Rice: The Origin of Rice Cultivation in the Americas* (Cambridge, MA: Harvard University Press, 2001), 1; Mart A. Stewart, "Slavery and the Origins of African American Environmentalism," in *"To Love the Wind and the Rain": African Americans and the Environment*, ed. Dianne D. Glave and Mark Stoll (Pittsburgh: University of Pittsburgh Press, 2006), 10–11.

8. Lou Ann Jones, *Mama Learned Us to Work: Farm Women in the New South* (Chapel Hill: University of North Carolina Press, 2002), 7.

9. Charles L. Perdue, Jr., Thomas E. Barden, and Robert K. Phillips, eds., *Weevils in the Wheat: Interviews with Virginia Ex-Slaves* (Charlottesville: University Press of Virginia, 1976), 247; Charles Joyner, *Down by the Riverside: A South Carolina Slave Community* (Urbana: University of Illinois Press, 1984), 14, 58; Mart A. Stewart, "Slavery and the Origins of African American Environmentalism," in *"To Love the Wind and the Rain": African Americans and the Environment*, ed. Dianne D. Glave and Mark Stoll (Pittsburgh: University of Pittsburgh Press, 2006), 12; Stewart, *"What Nature Suffers to Groe,"* 135; Joseph E. Holloway, ed.,

Africanisms in American Culture (Bloomington: University of Indiana Press, 1990), xii, 15–16; Lawrence W. Levine, *Black Culture and Black Consciousness: Afro-American Folk Thought from Slavery to Freedom* (New York: Oxford University Press, 1977), 61–62; Perdue, et al, *Weevils in the Wheat*, 266.

10. W. E. B. DuBois, *Black Reconstruction in America: An Essay Toward a History of the Part Which Black Folk Played in the Attempt to Reconstruct Democracy in America, 1860–1880* (New York: Russell & Russell, 1963); Eric Foner, *Reconstruction: America's Unfinished Revolution, 1863–1877* (New York: Harper and Row, 1988).

11. John Dittmer, *Black Georgia in the Progressive Era, 1900–1920* (Urbana: University of Illinois Press, 1977), 23; Manning Marable, "The Land Question in Historical Perspective: The Economics of Poverty in the Blackbelt South, 1865–1920," in *The Black Rural Landowner: Endangered Species; Social, Political, and Economic Implications*, eds. Leo McGee and Robert Boone. (Westport, CT: Greenwood Press, 1979), 3; Carter G. Woodson, *The Rural Negro* (New York: Russell and Russell, 1969), 47.

12. W. E. B. DuBois, *The Quest of the Silver Fleece* (New York: Arno Press, 1969), 31.

13. Ibid., *The Souls of Black Folk*, 123–24, 128.

14. James L. Wilson, *Clementine Hunter: American Folk Artist* (Gretna, LA: Pelican Publishing, 1988), 9, 19, 100–01; Shelby R. Gilley, *Painting by Heart: The Life and Art of Clementine Hunter, Louisiana Folk Artist* (Baton Rouge: St. Emma Press, 2000), 88.

15. "General Farm Notes: Controlling Insects," *The Negro Farmer* (April 1914).

16. Theodore Rosengarten, *All God's Dangers: The Life of Nate Shaw.* (New York: Vintage Books, 1989), 221–23.

17. Ibid., 224; Albert E. Cowdrey, *This Land, This South: An Environmental History* (Lexington: University Press of Kentucky, 1996), 110.

18. Rosengarten, *All God's Dangers*, 224.

19. Richard Bush Woodford, "Rotation of Crops and its Relation to Soil Fertility," *Southern Workman* XXXI, no. 6 (1903): 358.

20. Edward P. Jones, *The Known World* (New York: Amistad, HarperCollins, 2003), 1–2; "SAAFON: Southeastern African American Farmers Organic Network," http://www.saafon.org/.

7   CHILDREN: DREAMING AND DANGER IN WOODS AND FIELDS

1. W. E. B. DuBois, *The Souls of Black Folk* (New York: Penguin Books, 1969), 150.

2. Elizabeth D. Blum, "Power, Danger, and Control: Slave Women's Perceptions of Wilderness in the Nineteenth Century," *Women's Studies* 31, no. 2 (2002): 250; Sharla M. Fett, *Working Cures: Healing, Health, and Power on the Southern Slave Plantations* (Chapel Hill: University of North Carolina Press, 2002), 70, 72, 81.

3. For children in slavery, see Wilma King, *Stolen Childhood: Slave Youth in Nineteenth-Century America* (Bloomington: Indiana University Press, 1994), 13, 157–58; Marie Jenkins Schwartz, *Born in Bondage: Growing Up Enslaved in the Antebellum South* (Cambridge, MA: Harvard University Press, 2000), 131, 135–36.

4. Theodore Rosengarten, comp. *All God's Dangers: The Life of Nate Shaw* (New York: Vintage Books, 1989), 221; Albert Cowdrey, *This Land, This South: An Environmental History* (Lexington: University Press of Kentucky, 1996), 110.

5. "Lizzie Davis, Ex-slave," Born to Slavery: Slave Narratives From the Federal Writers Project, 1936–1938, Alabama Narratives, South Carolina Narratives, Volume XIV, Part 1, American Memory, Library of Congress, http://memory.log.gov, 293–94.

6. "Class in Nature Study," 1904, Digital ID 52631, http://digitalgallery.nypl.org; "Teach the Child Something about Real Country Life,"

1904, Digital ID 52633, http://digitalgallery.nypl.org; "Class in Out-door Nature," 1904, Digital ID 52620, http://digitalgallery.nypl.org; "'The Children's House': Class in Nature Study," 1904, Digital ID 52631, http://digitalgallery.nypl.org; "Whittier School students on a field trip studying plants, Hampton, Virginia," 1899, Reproduction Number LC-USZ62-38147, Prints and Photographs On-Line, Library of Congress, http://www.loc.gov/rr/print/catalog.html.

7. Beth E. Van Horn, Constance A. Flanagan, and Joan S. Thomson, "The First Fifty Years of the 4-H Program," *Journal of Extension* 36, no. 6 (December 1998), http://www.joe.org/joe/1998december/comm2 .html; Franklin M. Reck, *The 4-H Story: A History of 4-H Club Work* (Ames: Iowa State College Press, 1951), 139–40.

8. "North Carolina Wildlife Conservation Camp for Negro 4-H Club Boys & Girls, July 15–18, 1940," Negro Annual Reports, 4-H Club Work, 1936–1662, North Carolina State University Archives and Special Collections.

9. "Fifth Annual State Wildlife Conservation Camp for Negro 4-H Members, August 13–16, 1945," Negro Annual Reports, 4-H Club Work, 1936–1962, North Carolina State University (hereafter NCSU).

10. "North Carolina Wildlife Conservation Camp for Negro 4-H Club Boys & Girls, July 15–18, 1940," NCSU; "Wildlife Conservation Conference for Negro 4-H Club Youth, July 27–30, 1942," Program, 4-H Club Work, 1936–1962, NCSU.

11. "Eighth Annual State Wildlife Conservation Camp for Negro 4-H Members, August 22–27, 1945," NCSU.

12. "Seventh Annual Wildlife Conservation Camp for Negro 4-H Members, June 9–14, 1947"; "Tenth Annual Wildlife Conservation Camp for Negro 4-H Members, May 28–June 2, 1951," NCSU.

13. "Wildlife Conservation Camp for Negro 4-H Club Youth, July 14–17, 1941," NCSU; "Eighth Annual State Wildlife Conservation Camp for Negro 4-H Members, August 22–27, 1945," NCSU.

14. Valerie Boyd, *Wrapped in Rainbows: The Life of Zora Neale Hurston* (New York: Scribner, 2003), 42; Zora Neale Hurston, *Dust in the Tracks on a Road: An Autobiography* (New York: HarperPerennial, 1995), 52. Boyd is often unable to specify dates throughout Hurston's biography, including this 1904 date, because Hurston often claimed to be ten years younger than her actual age.

8   NATURE STUDY: OBSERVING, CLASSIFYING, AND UTILIZING THE NATURAL WORLD

1. Ralph Lutts, *The Nature Fakers: Wildlife, Science, and Sentiment* (Golden, CO: Fulcrum, 1990), 25, 27.

2. Marcia Myers Bonta, "Anna Botsford Comstock: Dean of American Nature Study," *Women in the Field: America's Pioneering Women Naturalists* (College Station: Texas A & M University Press, 1992), 154, 160, 165; Pamela M. Henson, "'Through Books to Nature': Anna Botsford Comstock and the Nature Study Movement," in *Natural Eloquence: Women Reinscribe Science*, ed. Barbara T. Gates and Ann B. Shteir (Madison: University of Wisconsin Press, 1997), 121, 125–27.

3. John H. Gehrs, *Agricultural Nature Study* (New York: American Books, 1929), 74.

4. Bonta, 160.

5. Alice Armstrong, review of *Nature Study and Life*, by Clifton H. Hodge, *Southern Workman* XXX, no. 5 (May 1902): 295; Clifton H. Hodge, *Nature Study and Life* (Boston: Ginn, 1902).

6. Letter to the Board of Education of the District of Columbia and General Education Board, "Statement of Hampton Summer School, 1903," VA 38, Hampton Institute, 1902–1905, General Education Board, Rockefeller Archive Center (hereafter known as GEB, RAC); Letter from H. B. Frissell, Secretary, Hampton Institute to Wallace Buttrick,

Secretary, GEB, RAC, November 9, 1903, VA 38, Hampton Institute, 1902–1905, GEB, RAC.

7. "Course in Primary Grades" (Hampton, VA: The Press of the Hampton Normal Agricultural Institute, c. 1900), The Hampton Leaflet Folder, "Bulletins, Circulars, Etc." Box, Hampton University Archival and Museum Collection (hereafter known HUAMC), 4–15.

8. "Hampton Nature-Study Leaflet" (Hampton, VA: The Press of the Hampton Normal Agricultural Institute, 1902), Extension Work Folder, "Bulletins, Circulars, Etc." Box, HUAMC, 4–7.

9. "Nature Study at Tuskegee," *The Tuskegee Student*, Saturday, October 29, 1904, Washington Collection, Special Collections, Tuskegee University; "Forty-First Annual Catalog: Tuskegee Normal and Industrial Institute, 1921–1922," 41, Tuskegee University, Washington Collection, Special Collections.

10. "Window Gardening for Schools: A Reference Text for Teachers," *Bulletin of the Florida Agricultural and Mechanical College for Negroes* 6, no. 1 (October 1913), Extension Department Folder, Bulletins, Circulars, Etc. Box, HUAMC, 5, 8–9, 12.

11. "Report of Slater Summer School, 1917," NC 236.4, Summer Schools, 1917–1927, VA 38, GEB, RAC; "Annual School Catalogue of St. Augustine's School, 1914," NC 121, St. Augustine College, 1903–1923, GEB, RAC.

12. Letter from Hollis B. Frissell, Hampton Institute, to Wallace Buttrick, General Education Board, n.d., VA 38, Hampton Institute, 1902–1905, GEB, RAC; Note from Hollis B. Frissell, Hampton Institute, to Wallace Buttrick, November 19, 1903, General Education Board, VA 38, Hampton Institute, October 20, 1902, 1902–1905, GEB, RAC.

13. Gloria Naylor, *Mama Day* (New York: Vintage Books, 1993), 1.

9   WOMEN AND GARDENING: A PATCH OF HER OWN

1. Alice Walker, *In Search of Our Mothers' Gardens* (San Diego: Harcourt Brace Jovanovich, 1983), 243.

2. Deborah Gray White, *Ar'n't I a Woman? Female Slaves in the Plantation South* (New York: W. W. Norton, 1999), 22, 155.

3. Thomas Monroe Campbell, *The Movable School Goes to the Negro Farmer* (Tuskegee, AL: Tuskegee Institute Press, 1936), 86.

4. Grey Gundaker, "Introduction: Home Ground," in *Keep Your Head to the Sky: Interpreting African American Home Ground*, ed. Grey Gundaker (Charlottesville: University Press of Virginia, 1998), 22.

5. Grey Gundaker, "African-American History, Cosmology, and the Moral Universe of Edward Houston's Yard," *Journal of Garden History* 14 (1994): 192, 197, 199; Ywone D. Edwards, "'Trash' Revisited: A Comparative Approach to Historical Descriptions and Archeological Analysis of Slave Houses and Yards," in *Keep Your Head to the Sky: Interpreting African American Home Ground*, ed. Grey Gundaker. (Charlottesville: University Press of Virginia, 1998), 264; Tom Hatley, "Tending Our Gardens," *Southern Changes* 6, no. 5 (July/August 1984): 18–24.

6. Zora Neale Hurston, "The Gilded Six Bits," in *The Norton Anthology: African American Literature*, ed. Henry Louis Gates Jr. and Nellie Y. McKay, (New York: W. W. Norton & Company, 1997), 10*ff.*; Gundaker, "African American History, Cosmology, and the Moral Universe," 179; Effie Graham, *The Passin'-on Party* (Chicago: McClurg, 1912), 24–25.

7. Richard Westmacott, "Yards and Gardens of Rural African Americans as Vernacular Art," *Southern Quarterly* 32 (Summer 1994): 54–55.

8. Vera Norwood, *Made from This Earth: American Women and Nature* (Chapel Hill: University of North Carolina Press, 1993), 136; Richard Westmacott, *African-American Gardens and Yards in the Rural South* (Knoxville: University of Tennessee Press, 1992), 108.

9. Elise Eugenia LeMaistre, "In Search of a Garden: African Americans and the Land in Piedmont Georgia." A.B. thesis, Princeton University, 1981), 37–55; Westmacott, *African-American Gardens and Yards*, 2, 54–55, 106–07.

10. Lewis W. Jones, "The South's Negro Farm Agent," *Journal of Negro Education* 38 (Winter 1953): 43; LeMaistre, "In Search of a Garden," 37–55; Westmacott, *African-American Gardens and Yards*, 54–55. Hatley, "Tending Our Gardens," 18–19.

11. John Michael Vlach, *The Back of the Big House: The Architecture of Plantation Slavery* (Chapel Hill: University of North Carolina Press, 1993), 166; Edwards, 247.

12. Jacqueline Jones, *Labor of Love, Labor of Sorrow: Black Women, Work, and the Family, from Slavery to Present* (New York: Vintage Books, 1985), 36; Jones "The South's Negro Farm Agent," 43; Vlach, *Back of the Big House*, 166; Casper Rumple, De Valls Bluff, Arkansas, "Born in Slavery: Slave Narratives from the Federal Writers' Project, 1936–1938," Arkansas Narratives, vol. II, Part 6, American Memory, Library of Congress, http://memory.loc.gov/ammem/snhtml/snhome.html, 104.

13. Glenda Elizabeth Gilmore, *Gender and Jim Crow: Women and the Politics of White Supremacy in North Carolina, 1896–1920* (Chapel Hill: University of North Carolina Press, 1996), 44; Jones, *Labor of Love*, 88; Westmacott, "Yards and Gardens," 55; Mary C. Gates, "Homes and Homemaking," *Southern Workman* no. 2 (February 1901): 121.

14. Westmacott, "Yards and Gardens," 54–55; Shelby R. Gilley, *Painting by Heart: The Life and Art of Clementine Hunter, Louisiana Folk Artist* (Baton Rouge: St. Emma Press, 2000), 76.

15. Gilley, 80.

16. Walker, 241.

17. Jones, *Labor of Love*, 86; LeMaistre, 43; Gretchen Lemke-Santangelo, *Abiding Courage: African American Migrant Women and the East Bay Community* (Chapel Hill: University of North Carolina Press, 1996), 139–40; Westmacott, "Yards and Gardens," 54.

18. Bernice L. McFadden, *Camilla's Roses* (New York: Dutton, Penguin Group, 2004), xii–xiii.

19. "Places for the Spirit: Traditional African American Gardens of the South," http://www.vaughnsills.com/gardens/gardens.html.

10 ENVIRONMENTAL JUSTICE: FREE TO BREATHE

1. "African American Denominational Leaders Pledge Their Support to the Struggle Against Environmental Racism," *The AME Christian Recorder* (May 18, 1998): 11.

2. Dwight N. Hopkins, *Introducing Black Theology of Liberation* (Maryknoll, NY: Orbis Books, 1999), 34; Martin Luther King Jr. "Letter from a Birmingham Jail," April 16, 1963, http://www.stanford.edu/group/King/frequentdocs/birmingham.pdf.

3. Robert Bullard, *Unequal Protection: Environmental Justice and Communities of Color* (New York: Random House, 1994), 3–4.

4. Cornell Christion, "The Memphis Sanitation Strike: Blood and Strife Brought Dignity for City Workers," *The Commercial Memphis*, February 28, 1993, http://www.newgomemphis.com/newgo/mlk/strike.html; "Memphis We Remember: 1968 Sanitation Workers' Strike Chronology," 2002, http://www.afscme.org/about/memphchr.htm.

5. "Memphis We Remember: 1968 Sanitation Workers' Strike Chronology."

6. "I've Been to the Mountaintop," April 3, 1968, http://mlk-kpp01.stanford.edu/index.php/encyclopedia/enclyclopedia/enc_ive_been_to_the_mountaintop_3_april_1968/; Melvin Dixon, *Ride Out the Wilderness: Geography and Identity in Afro-American Literature* (Urbana: University of Illinois Press, 1987), 1.

7. "National Black Church Environmental and Economic Justice Summit," 14.

8. Eileen McGurty, *Transforming Environmentalism: Warren County, PCBs, and the Origins of Environmental Justice* (Rutgers: Rutgers University Press, 2007), 301; Anthony B. Pinn, *The Black Church in the Post-Civil Rights Era* (Maryknoll, NY: Orbis Books, 2002), 84–85.

9. "A Salute to the Commission for Racial Justice," *New York Voice Inc./ Harlem USA* 42, no. 13 (July 5, 2000), 4.

10. United Church of Christ, *Toxic Wastes and Race in the United States: A National Report on the Racial and Socio-economic Characteristics of Communities with Hazardous Waste Sites* (New York: Public Data Access, 1987), x; "A Salute to the Commission for Racial Justice," 4.

11. "National Black Church Environmental and Economic Justice Summit," 24–26; "Jesus People Against Pollution," http://www.universityof thepoor.org/campaign/orgs/jpap.html.

12. Martha Kendrick Cobb, "The Legacy of a Trio of Justice Seekers," United Church of Christ, *Witness for Justice*, May, 20, 2002, http://www .ucc.org/justice/witness/wfj052002.htm; "'Toxic Tour' Marks 15th Anniversary," *United Church News*, June 2002, http://www.ucc.org/ ucnews/jun02/toxic.htm.

13. Anthony Pinn, *The Black Church in the Post-Civil Rights Era* (Mary Knoll, NY: Orbis Books, 2002), 86–87.

14. Cone, "Whose Earth Is It Anyway?"; "National Black Church Environmental and Economic Justice Summit," 3.

15. "African American Denominational Leaders Pledge Their Support to the Struggle Against Environmental Racism," 8, 11.

16. Alexander Crummell, "Incidents of Hope for the Negro Race in America: A Thanksgiving Sermon, November 26th, 1895," Library of Congress, http://memory.loc.gov/cgibin/ampage?collId=ody_ rbcmisc&fileName=ody/ody0612/ody0612page.db&recNum= 2&itemLink=%2Fammem%2Faaohtml%2Fexhibit%2Faopart6 .html%230612&linkText=9; Allen Freeman Davis, *Spearheads for Reform: The Social Settlements and the Progressive Movement, 1890–1914* (New York: Oxford University Press, 1967).

CONCLUSION: HERITAGE AND THE FUTURE

1. "New Energy for America," http://www.barackobama.com/issues/ newenergy/index.php.
2. "Obama's Speech to the Copenhagen Summit," http://www.guardian .co.uk/environment/2009/dec/18/obama-speech-copenhagen-climate -summit.

Further Reading

Blum, Elizabeth D. *Love Canal Revisited: Race, Class, and Gender in Environmental Activism*. Lawrence: University Press of Kansas, 2008.

Carney, Judith A. *Black Rice: The African Origins of Rice Cultivation in the Americas*. Cambridge, MA: Harvard University Press, 2001.

Deming, Alison H. and Lauret E. Savoy, eds. *The Colors of Nature: Culture, Identity, and the Natural World*. Minneapolis, MN: Milkweed Editions, 2002.

Dungy, Camille T., ed. *Black Nature: Four Centuries of African American Nature Poetry*. Athens: University of Georgia Press, 2009.

Edmondson, Dudley. *The Black & Brown Faces in America's Wild Places: African Americans Making Nature and the Environment a Part of Their Everyday Lives*. Cambridge, MN: Adventure Publications, Inc., 2006.

Glave, Dianne and Mark Stoll, ed. *"To Love the Wind and the Rain": African Americans and Environmental History*. Pittsburgh, PA: University of Pittsburgh Press, 2006.

Gundaker, Grey and Judith McWillie. *No Space Hidden: The Spirit of African American Yard Work*. Knoxville: University of Tennessee Press, 2005.

Horne, Jed. *Breach of Faith: Hurricane Katrina and the Near Death of a Great American City.* New York: Random House, 2008.

Hurley, Andrew. *Environmental Inequalities: Class, Race, and Industrial Pollution in Gary, Indiana, 1945–1980.* Chapel Hill: University of North Carolina Press, 1995.

Johnson, Shelton. *Gloryland: A Novel.* San Francisco: Sierra Club/Counterpoint, 2009.

Peterman, Audrey and Frank Peterman. *Legacy on the Land: A Black Couple Discovers Our National Inheritance and Tells Why Every American Should Care.* Atlanta: Earthwise Productions, Inc., 2009.

Proctor, Nicolas W. *Bathed in Blood: Hunting and Mastery in the Old South.* Charlottesville: University of Virginia Press, 2002.

Shackel, Paul A. *Memory in Black and White: Race, Commemoration, and the Post-Bellum Landscape.* Walnut Creek, CA: Altamira Press, 2003.

Smith, Kimberly K. *African American Environmental Thought: Foundations.* Lawrence: University Press of Kansas, 2007.

Stewart, Mart A. *"What Nature Suffers to Groe": Life, Labor, and Landscape on the Georgia Coast, 1680–1920.* Athens: University of Georgia Press, 1996.

Photo Credits

PAGE 1: State Archives of Florida

PAGE 2: Photographs and Prints Division, Schomburg Center for Research in Black Culture, the New York Public Library, Astor, Lenox and Tilden Foundations

PAGE 3: (top) Robert N. Dennis Collection of Stereoscopic Views, Miriam and Ira D. Wallach Division of Arts, Prints and Photographs, the New York Public Library, Astor, Lenox and Tilden Foundations; (middle) Photographs and Prints Division, Schomburg Center for Research in Black Culture, the New York Public Library, Astor, Lenox and Tilden Foundations; (bottom) General Research & Reference Division, Schomburg Center for Research in Black Culture, the New York Public Library, Astor, Lenox and Tilden Foundations

PAGE 4: (top) Seeds of Change: The Daily Reflector Image Collection, J. Y. Joyner Library, East Carolina University, Greenville, N.C., http://digital.lib.ecu.edu/2703; (middle) "Girl Scout First Aid," Seeds of Change: The Daily Reflector Image Collection, J. Y. Joyner Library, East Carolina

Index

Dianne D. Glave teaches in the Department of History at Morehouse College, the
only all-men's Historically Black College
and University. The coeditor of *"To Love the
Wind and the Rain": African Americans and
Environmental History*, she has a doctorate
in U.S. social history with an emphasis
on African American and environmental
history. She recently received her M.Div.
focusing on faith, health, and science. Her articles on the environ-
ment have appeared in various publications, including *Environmental
History*. She lives in Atlanta.